LIVING
TRUTH

THE KEYS TO SHEDDING IDEALS

LIVING

AND EXPECTATIONS TO FIND

TRUTH

AUTHENTIC  SUCCESS

SUCCESS
BOOKS®
Lake Mary, FL

CONTENTS

CHAPTER 1

LIVING YOUR AUTHENTIC SELF

By Jack Canfield

To be nobody but yourself in a world which is doing
its best day and night to make you like every-
body else means to fight the hardest battle.
—E. E. CUMMINGS

When I was in my midtwenties, I stood nervously in front of a classroom full of inner-city African American high school students, armed only with an undergraduate degree in Chinese history, one year of mostly academic teacher training in a yet-to-be-completed master's degree program, and very little experience in teaching teenagers. It was 1968, the world was shifting beneath our feet, and there I was, teaching in Chicago at Calumet High School, trying to make history relevant to kids who were more concerned with dating and surviving the streets than understanding the five causes of the Civil War, let alone facts about the Ming Dynasty.

It was in that humble classroom, under fluorescent lights and against the backdrop of chalkboard dust and adolescent apathy, that I first understood what it meant to show up as yourself, fully, unapologetically, and vulnerably.

Not as "Mr. Canfield, the teacher." Not as "Jack, the white guy in a suit and tie with a BA in history from Harvard riding in on a white horse with a perfectly developed lesson plan," but as a human being with a heart that beat just as theirs did, with dreams and insecurities and a deep longing to connect.

I remember one particular day when my carefully prepared lesson on the Industrial Revolution was met with vacant stares and restless shuffling. I had been trying so hard to be the perfect teacher—the one who had all the answers, who could command respect through my superior knowledge and my position of authority.

It all changed one day when one of my students raised his hand and said, "You have a college degree from Harvard. You could have done anything you wanted—become a lawyer or a doctor, or gone to work for a big company and made a lot of money. Why did you choose to become a teacher in a Black school with us?" He was looking for an honest answer—not some platitude or canned response.

I put down my textbook and said, "You know what? I wanted to do something with my life that mattered. I wanted to make a difference, to contribute something meaningful to people who needed support to succeed. But I need your help to make that happen. Sometimes I am scared that I am not reaching you, that what I am teaching is not that relevant, that what I am teaching you is not what you really need."

The room went silent. Then something beautiful happened. A hand went up. Then another. And for the next hour we had the most honest conversation about what the truth of our situation was. "I appreciate you coming here with a commitment to truly make a difference in our lives. It seems like a lot of other teachers are just going through the motions. It's like they don't even want to be here." (The fact was that most teachers in that school would have rather been teaching in an all-White school in the suburbs.) "Why doesn't our textbook contain anything about Black history?" I asked if they could learn about anything, what they would like to learn.

We ended up talking about racism, the Civil Rights Movement, the fear of gang violence, (we had two warring gangs in our school—the Devil's Disciples and the Blackstone Rangers), drugs, the fact that our school didn't have a football team or a swim team, and many other similar issues.

That day changed everything—not because I had finally found the right teaching technique but because I had finally found the courage to drop my lesson plan and be real. It was there, in that dusty classroom, that I first learned an essential truth: If you want to reach people, if you want to make a real impact, you need to show up fully, unapologetically, and authentically—not as some role you think you have to play to gain respect, approval, inclusion, popularity, or love.

As a result of that day's authentic conversation, I bought all the students a paperback copy of *Before the Mayflower: A History of the Negro in America, 1619–1962* by Lerone Bennet, and started teaching African American history, along with the prescribed textbook. I began to take the first ten minutes of every class and lead the students through a self-esteem-building exercise. Having been on the swim team in high school and been a certified water-safety instructor and swim teacher at a summer camp, I worked with a physical-education teacher to start Calumet's first swim team. I was asked by the student body to be the faculty adviser for the first African-American Society club, and I was voted Teacher of the Year by the student body—in my first year of teaching!

THE MASKS WE WEAR

From the moment we are born, most of us are taught to wear masks. As kids, we learn that if we say the right thing, act the right way, and follow all the rules, we'll be liked, accepted, and maybe even loved. The problem is, we start to confuse the mask for our identity. We forget who we are underneath.

I wore a lot of masks early in my life. The good son. The straight-A student. The guy who could hold it together no matter what. I was driven to succeed, but underneath that drive there was always the fear that I was not enough. That if people saw the real me, the one who felt too sensitive, too idealistic, too different, they'd reject me.

Growing up in a middle-class family in Wheeling, West Virginia, I learned early on that vulnerability was weakness. My father was a workaholic who showed love through providing economically, not through emotional connection. My mother was so focused on maintaining appearances that genuine feelings were often swept under the rug in favor of social acceptability.

I became a master of reading rooms, of becoming whoever I thought people wanted me to be. In high school I was the academic achiever with the teachers, the class clown with my friends, and the dutiful son at home. By the time I graduated, I was exhausted, though I couldn't have told you why.

It wasn't until I started doing the deep work on myself—therapy, personal development seminars, spiritual retreats—that I began peeling back those layers. Each time I took off a mask, it felt risky. But every time I did, just like that day in the classroom, I discovered something profound: Authenticity is magnetic. It's the foundation of true connection and real intimacy, and the key to inner peace, happiness, and fulfillment.

The Price of Pretending

There's a cost to inauthenticity. It's not always visible at first, but it accumulates. It shows up as anxiety, depression, burnout, physical pain, and even chronic illness. It fractures relationships. It leads to a life that looks good on the outside but feels empty and hollow on the inside.

I've coached thousands of people over the years—CEOs, sales teams, stay-at-home moms, high school students—and I can tell you this: The pain of pretending is universal. So is the longing to come home to ourselves.

In one of my Breakthrough to Success trainings a participant who was a doctor complained that he suffered from regular and painful migraine headaches. I asked him to close his eyes and imagine that he was his headache. I asked him, "What does your headache want to say to you? What message does it want you to hear?" The headache told him, "I am a constant reminder that you are not doing what you want to do in life. I am trying to get your attention to tell you how much pain you are in from not pursuing your real dream."

He went on to explain that everyone in his family was a doctor— both of his parents, his aunt and uncle, and his older brother and sister. He was *expected* to become a doctor. His passion was working on high-end foreign cars. His family thought that being a "mechanic" was a "lower-class blue-collar job," one beneath their family image. As a result of our session, he went home, quit his job as an anesthesiologist, and opened a garage for repairing and maintaining luxury cars, and his headaches permanently disappeared. He also later reported that he was making just as much money as he was as a doctor and was much happier than he had ever been.

THE HIGH PRICE OF PEOPLE-PLEASING

True joy and happiness can only be found by loving yourself, going inward, following your heart, and doing what brings you joy.

—ANITA MOORJANI

Three years ago I read *Dying to Be Me*, Anita Moorjani's memoir, in which she describes the near-death experience she had during her life-threatening battle with end-stage lymphoma and the profound lessons she learned. She recounts the details of her childhood in a traditional Indian family and her struggle to find her true self amid the strong cultural, religious, and familial expectations she faced, and how that led to her near-fatal illness.

Lying in the hospital, weighing a mere eighty pounds with tumors the size of golf balls, her body had stopped absorbing nutrition, her lungs were filled with fluid, and her muscles had completely deteriorated, leaving her resembling a skeleton unable to move. When she was expected to die any day, she fell into a coma and had a near-death experience where she was transported to a realm where she experienced unconditional love for her true self and a state of expanded awareness, in which she realized that the cause of her cancer was her fear and lack of self-love, which stemmed from a lifetime of suppressing her authentic self in order to meet other people's expectations. Upon regaining consciousness, she experienced a rapid and complete remission, defying all medical expectations. In her book she emphasized the importance of self-love, living fearlessly, and embracing one's unique self as the paths to healing and experiencing a fulfilling life. She wrote that while she was in the state of unconditional love and awareness, "I somehow knew in some way, that I was meant to inspire thousands....I just had to be myself and enjoy life, and to allow myself to be an instrument for something much bigger to take place."

Staying True to Yourself Creates Miracles

I often say that if I had a prayer, it would be this: God, spare me from the desire for love, approval, or appreciation.
—Byron Katie

In 1994 Oprah Winfrey's daytime talk show ratings were slipping. Overwhelmed by the pressure to chase ratings with shows on sensational topics, she was exhausted and burned out. It is reported that she even fainted on set due to her sheer exhaustion and emotional depletion.

She later said the reason was that she was in a deep misalignment with her values and her soul just to stay on top of the ratings. Choosing to proceed more authentically, she told her producers: "I am no longer going to do shows that make me feel bad about myself. I don't care what the ratings say."

From that moment on she began producing shows that aligned with *her true values*. She started interviewing people and doing stories that were more positive, inspiring, healing, and uplifting, featuring people such as John Gray, the author of *Men Are from*

Mars, Women Are from Venus, and books and movies such as *The Secret*, which introduced the nation to the Law of Attraction, that show featuring me, Rhonda Byrne, Lisa Nichols, and Rev. Michael Bernard Beckwith.

As a result of honoring her true self, the show climbed in popularity again—because people felt her authenticity and the depth of the content. This complete reset went on to later become the foundation for Super Soul Sunday, and The Oprah Winfrey Network—OWN.

Oprah later said, "When I aligned with my truth, the miracles followed."

THE TURNING POINT: CHICKEN SOUP FOR THE SOUL

When Mark Victor Hansen and I coauthored the first *Chicken Soup for the Soul*® book, we didn't know we were building a brand that would ultimately sell more than five hundred million books worldwide. We just wanted to share stories that mattered—real, heart-centered stories that reminded people of the good in themselves and the world.

The idea was simple: collect true stories that inspired, uplifted, and healed. What wasn't simple was getting anyone to publish it. We were rejected by 144 publishers. We were told the book was too sentimental and that no one would read a book with the title *Chicken Soup for the Soul*, that people didn't want feel-good stories. One editor actually said, "The book is too positive, too Pollyanna."

But Mark and I knew the power of the stories we had. We had been telling them in our talks and workshops, and people were always moved and inspired by them. What I didn't expect was how much resistance we'd face, not just from publishers but once the book was finally published, from the literary establishment. Some people dismissed the books as "pop psychology" and "emotional manipulation."

But then the letters started coming. Thousands of them. From people whose lives had been changed by reading about someone else's true-life experiences—tales of acts of kindness, love, and generosity. Stories of courage and overcoming fear. Stories of everyday people just like them overcoming what seemed like insurmountable obstacles. Stories of faith and miracles.

We eventually received more than two thousand letters just from teenagers who decided not to end their lives because they read about how someone like them had overcome similar experiences of rejection, failure, self-judgment, and despair. We also received letters from couples who were able to save their marriages because they found hope in another couple's story of forgiveness and redemption.

These deeply personal stories resonated with people because they were authentic and vulnerable. Psychologist Carl Rogers once said, "What is most personal is most universal." And this insight was proved to be true by the millions of readers who were moved by the honesty and the transparency of these simple but profound stories.

THE INNER JOURNEY

Living authentically isn't a one-time choice. It's a moment-by-moment practice. It's about aligning your outer expression with your inner truth.

For me, that's looked like turning down speaking gigs that didn't align with my values, even when the potential paycheck was big. I once walked away from a six-figure contract because the company wanted me to endorse practices I couldn't stand behind.

It's looked like saying, "I don't know," when I didn't have the answer, even when people expected me to be the expert. This was particularly hard early in my career, when I felt like I had to have all the answers to be credible.

It's looked like crying in front of an audience when a story touched me deeply, even when I initially feared looking weak. The first time this happened, I was terribly uncomfortable. But the response from the audience taught me that vulnerability creates connection, not distance.

It's looked like being willing to admit my mistakes publicly. I've failed at businesses, been divorced, made poor investment decisions, and sometimes given advice that didn't serve people as well as I had hoped. Owning these failures hasn't diminished my credibility; it's enhanced it.

I've had to learn to trust that who I am is enough. And that the more I show up as myself, the more I give others permission to do the same.

PERMISSION TO BE YOU

Here's the truth: You don't need to earn the right to be yourself. You were born with that right. But many of us are waiting for someone to grant us permission. To say it's safe. To say it's OK. So let me say it now, if no one ever has: You have permission to be who you are. To speak your truth. To follow what lights you up. To let go of what no longer fits. To disappoint others rather than betray yourself.

You don't have to fit in. You were born to stand out.

This permission isn't a one-time gift. It's something you also have to give yourself again and again, especially when the world tries to squeeze you back into its comfortable boxes.

LIVING LEGACY

As I reflect on my life, the stages I've stood on, the books I've written, and the people I've mentored, I realize that the greatest thing I've ever done is give people the tools and courage to be themselves—not the selves they thought they should be but the selves they are.

When we live in alignment with our true nature, everything else falls into place. We find the right work, the right relationships, the right rhythm. We stop chasing approval and start living a life of purpose. This doesn't mean life always becomes easy. It means it becomes real. And real, while sometimes difficult, is always more satisfying than fake.

So How Do You Start?

Here are a few practical steps to begin or deepen your journey into authenticity:

- **Tell yourself the truth.** Get honest with yourself. What are you pretending not to know? What are you tolerating that's draining your soul? Start a truth journal where you write down one honest thing about yourself each day.

- **Get still.** Spend time in silence each day. Listen. Your authentic self whispers before it roars. Even five minutes of quiet reflection can help you reconnect with your inner voice.

- **Take off the mask.** Share something real with someone you trust. Let yourself be seen. Vulnerability is your superpower, not your weakness.

- **Follow your joy.** What lights you up? What do you lose track of time doing? That's your soul talking. Listen. Make space in your life for more of what energizes you.

- **Honor your values.** Identify your core values, and use them as a compass for decision-making. When you're aligned with your values, authenticity becomes much, much easier.

- **Surround yourself with truth tellers.** Build a circle of people who see you, accept you, challenge you, and reflect you back to yourself. Distance yourself from those who want you to be someone you're not.

- **Practice the Mirror Exercise.** Every morning, look yourself in the eye and ask: "How can I show up more authentically today?" Listen for the answer.

- **Practice the Evening Review.** This powerful exercise will help you accelerate the practice of authenticity in your day-to-day life. You'll be amazed at how fast this technique can lead to a permanent change. I highly recommend that you do this exercise at the end of the day or your workday for a minimum of thirty days in a row. Sit with your eyes closed, take a few deep cleansing breaths, and give one of the following instructions to your higher self, spirit guide, guardian angel, or God:
  - Show me where I could have been more authentic today.
  - Show me where I could have expressed more authenticity today.
  - Show me where I could have been more open and vulnerable today.
  - Show me where I could have been more transparent in my communication today.
  - Show me where I could have been more assertive in expressing my true needs today.
  - Show me where I could have been more assertive in saying no today.

As you sit calmly in a state of quiet receptivity, you'll see that a number of events from the day will come to mind. Just observe them without any judgment or self-criticism. When no more events come to mind, take each incident and replay it in your mind the way you would have preferred to have acted had you been more conscious and intentional at the time. This creates a subconscious image that will help evoke the desired behavior more easily the next time you find yourself in a similar situation.

FINAL THOUGHTS

Living and expressing your authentic self isn't always easy. It requires courage, discernment, and sometimes letting go of people, places, and patterns that no longer serve you. But it's worth it.

The world doesn't need more polished, perfect personas. It needs you. The real you. The one who laughs too loud. Who feels deeply. Who dreams big. Who shows up with an open heart and says, "This is me." And that's the person who changes the world. And that's the legacy worth living.

After more than five decades of teaching, speaking, and writing about success, I can tell you this with absolute certainty: Your authenticity is not just your gift to yourself; it's your gift to the world. Every time you choose to be real instead of perfect, you give someone else permission to do the same.

And that's how we heal the world, one authentic moment at a time.

About Jack

Known as America's #1 Success Coach, Jack Canfield is the founder and chairman of the Canfield Training Group in Santa Barbara, California, which trains and coaches entrepreneurs, corporate leaders, managers, sales professionals, educators, and the general public in how to accelerate the achievement of their personal, professional, and financial goals.

Jack Canfield is best known as the coauthor of the number one *New York Times* best-selling Chicken Soup for the Soul® book series, which has sold more than six hundred million books in forty-nine languages, including forty-one *New York Times* best sellers.

As the CEO of Chicken Soup for the Soul Enterprises, he helped grow the Chicken Soup for the Soul® brand into a virtual empire of books, children's books, audios, videos, CDs, classroom materials, a syndicated column, and a television show, as well as a vigorous program of licensed products that includes everything from clothing and board games to nutraceuticals and a successful line of Chicken Soup for the Pet Lover's Soul® cat and dog foods.

His other books include *The Success Principles™: How to Get from Where You Are to Where You Want to Be* (now available in its 20th Anniversary Edition); *The Success Principles Workbook*; *The Success Principles for Teens*; *The Aladdin Factor*; *Dare to Win*; *Heart at Work*; *The Power of Focus: How to Hit Your Personal, Financial and Business Goals with Absolute Certainty*; *You've Got to Read This Book*; *Tapping into Ultimate Success*; *Jack Canfield's Key to Living the Law of Attraction*; *The 30-Day Sobriety Solution*; and his autobiographical novel, *The Golden Motorcycle Gang: A Story of Transformation*.

Jack is a dynamic speaker and was inducted into the National Speakers Association's Speaker Hall of Fame. He has appeared on more than one thousand radio and television shows, including *Oprah*, *Montel*, *Larry King Live*, *The Today Show*, *Fox and Friends*, and two different hour-long *PBS Specials* devoted exclusively to his work. Jack is also a featured teacher in twelve movies, including *The Secret*, *The Meta-Secret*, *The Truth*, *The Keeper of the Keys*, *Tapping into the Source*, and *The Tapping Solution*. Jack was also honored with a documentary produced about his life and teachings called *The Soul of Success: The Jack Canfield Story*.

Jack has personally helped hundreds of thousands of people on six continents become multimillionaires, business leaders, best-selling authors, leading sales professionals, successful entrepreneurs, and world-class athletes while at the same time creating balanced, fulfilling, and healthy lives.

His corporate clients have included Virgin Records, SONY Pictures, Daimler-Chrysler, Federal Express, GE, Johnson & Johnson, Microsoft, Merrill Lynch, Campbell's Soup, Re/Max, The Million Dollar Forum, The Million Dollar Roundtable, The Young Entrepreneurs Organization, The Young Presidents Organization, the Executive Committee, and the World Business Council.

He is the founder of the Transformational Leadership Council and a member of Evolutionary Leaders, two groups devoted to helping create a world that works for everyone.

Jack is a graduate of Harvard, earned his MEd from the University of Massachusetts, and has received three honorary doctorates in psychology and public service. He is married and has three children, two stepchildren, and two grandsons.

For more information, visit:

- www.JackCanfield.com

CHAPTER 2

UNCOMPROMISED

*How Desire, Conviction, and Purpose
Point Us to Who We Really Are*

———————

By Nick Nanton

They say the truth will set you free. What they don't say is how often it'll try to run from you first. How it'll morph under the pressure of criticism, or how it'll whisper in one moment and scream at you the next.

My life—the businesses I've built, the films I've directed, the people I've stood beside—has been a continual confrontation with truth. And every time I reached a new level of success or significance, it came with a choice—not between right and wrong but between being liked and being honest. Between comfort and alignment. Between the story others expected me to live and the one I knew I had to tell.

As a director, an entrepreneur, and a guy who's sat across from people such as Larry King, Dolly Parton, and everyday heroes with impossible stories, the truth hasn't just been a theme; it has been a test. Over and over again. There were moments I could have played it safe and told the story people *wanted* to hear. There were deals on the table that would've meant more money, more press, more comfort, if only I'd diluted the message. But I couldn't. I've built a life and a legacy on capturing what's *real*, and that meant I had to *live* real too. That meant standing by my truth even when it was inconvenient or unpopular.

What I have learned is that there is a high cost but an even higher reward of telling the unvarnished truth. I've also learned, sometimes the hard way, how to identify it, stand by it, and build a life worth filming, by living a truth worth telling.

Truth Begins with Desire

Before I knew what living my truth really meant, I knew what I wanted it to be. I was trying to build a reputation in multiple industries, and I wanted to be *seen*. I wanted to be *validated*. I knew I had something to offer the world, but I had to get invited to the proverbial party. I had written songs, and while I believed they were good, no one was handing me a Grammy. I got tired of waiting on the Grammys, so I did what any restless creative would do: I googled "how to win an Emmy." Ridiculous? Maybe. But that search changed my life.

At the time, I was fully immersed in the business world, traveling the country as an entertainment attorney and a keynote speaker, growing my company with my business partner, and hosting events for high-level entrepreneurs and experts who wanted to grow their businesses. I understood the power of third-party credibility. I knew what credentials could do for someone's career and how one well-placed accolade could shortcut a decade of knocking on doors. I had helped other people do it.

I wasn't chasing an award just for ego's sake. I was chasing a *future*. I knew I was a creator. I knew I had something to say, and I was ready to prove it. The first step to winning an Emmy, according to the internet, was to find a compelling story to tell. What I've learned since then is that you *feel* your truth long before you can articulate it. It shows up in desire. Quietly. Persistently. It doesn't scream; it *pulls*. You find truth not by shouting, "Who am I?" into the void but by following the breadcrumbs and trusting that even the most unconventional urges are leading you somewhere honest. For me, the breadcrumb trail led to the desire to win an Emmy and to a chance meeting with a stranger in an airport.

I was sitting next to a man and noticed he was flipping through pictures on his computer. There was a smiling little boy with

Down syndrome in several of them. The man told me it was his son. We talked for a bit, and we exchanged information as he had asked me if I could help get some items from famous bands for a charity auction to support Down syndrome. A few months later he emailed me an article his wife had written about their son's love of baseball. When the article arrived in my inbox, I forwarded it to my dad and my business partner. They were so taken with it that they shared it with a few people, who shared it with a few more. Before I knew it, this moving story about a boy and a baseball field had touched more hearts than I could count.

And that's when I knew, *this* was the story.

That experience lit something in me I couldn't unfeel. The moment I began producing what would become an Emmy Award–winning documentary called *Jacob's Turn*, I felt a part of myself unlock. My heart exploded. My creativity was on fire. And more than anything else, I felt aligned. I knew without a doubt that making movies was going to be a part of my life no matter what. That was the next layer of my truth: I was, and had always been, a storyteller—not just in the artistic sense but in the soul sense. And there was no going back.

Truth Awakens Purpose

There are moments in life when your truth demands more than words. It calls for action, even when the stakes are high. For me, that moment came with the documentary *Brisa*, a project that tested the very core of my convictions. There are times when living your truth isn't just uncomfortable; it's dangerous. That was the case when I said yes to telling the story of Brisa De Angulo.

Brisa is a survivor. At just fifteen, she endured one of the most brutal violations a person can experience and then survived the injustice that followed. The Bolivian courts failed her. The legal system re-traumatized her. Her home was even set on fire in retaliation for speaking out. But she refused to stay quiet. Instead, she transformed her pain into purpose. Brisa became a lawyer. She founded *A Breeze of Hope*, the first center in Bolivia dedicated to helping child survivors of sexual violence. And she took her case to the Inter-American Court of Human Rights, where in a landmark decision she won. The court admonished the Bolivian government for its civil and human rights violations. The ruling set precedent not just for Bolivia but for the entire region. Because of Brisa the world was forced to pay attention.

When I chose to make a documentary about her journey, I knew there were real risks. Powerful forces were at play. They were the kind of cartel-level forces that might make most people step back and say, "This isn't my fight." But how could I stay out of it when it was clearly the right thing to do? Brisa had given her life to protecting children. She had faced threats, loss, and betrayal, and her commitment changed lives. What kind of storyteller would I be if I backed away from that? That project taught me something I carry with me every day: If you want to live your truth, you must be willing to risk comfort for conviction. You must make your purpose bigger than your fear. The world doesn't need more people playing it safe. It needs more people telling the truth even when it's dangerous. So the question is, What truth have you been avoiding because it feels too risky to tell? And what might change if you made your purpose bigger than your fear? You may not be called to face global powers, but you are being called to something. Are you willing to follow it, even when it's uncomfortable? Sometimes the most powerful way to honor your truth is to simply have the courage not to look away from it.

TRUTH CLARIFIES YOUR VALUES

Living your truth sounds noble in theory, but in real life it often shows up as a quiet *no*. It's not always a dramatic decision. Sometimes it's a line in a script, a tone that doesn't sit right in your gut.

I was in early talks to make a movie with someone I respected. The concept was solid, but as we started digging into the script, something felt off. There were more nude scenes than necessary and more profanity than served the story. When I asked about it, the answer was one you hear all the time in entertainment: "That's just how it is." But it's not how it is for *me*.

I've worked too hard to build a life around meaning to now attach my name to something that doesn't reflect my values. I told them if that was the direction they were going, I didn't want to be involved, not out of judgment but out of alignment.

I've had to pump the brakes more than once when the direction of a project didn't resonate with *my* purpose, *my* goals, or *my* brand of impact. A lot of filmmakers think you need swearing and nudity to hold an audience's attention. I don't believe that. But I also don't believe in hyper-sanitizing life to make it palatable for everyone. The power, I've found, is in balance. It's in telling stories that are raw but respectful, emotionally rich but not exploitative. Stories that don't rely on extremes to feel true. That's what values do. They help you recognize what's yours and what's not. They give you the courage to walk away from something good so you can say yes to something great. And they anchor you when everything else—the money, the recognition, the fast track—tries to pull you off course. The truth isn't just what you say. It's what you stand for, especially when no one's watching.

So let me ask you, Where in your life or work are you compromising on something that quietly betrays your values? And what would it feel like to stand firm instead?

YOUR TRUTH IS IN YOUR GIFTS

One of the most surprising things about living your truth is this: It rarely looks the way you *expect* it to. Sometimes it doesn't look like some grand transformation or radical change. Sometimes truth is simply about finally respecting what's *already inside you*.

I have a friend whose work is about revolutionizing company culture. He builds systems and structures that make space for better communication, healthier leadership, and more inspired teams. It's transformative work. But over coffee one day he said something that stopped me: "I just wish I could do something more creative." I almost laughed, not at him but at the irony.

The way he weaves human behavior, communication, and operational design together *is* creativity. That *is* art. But because it didn't look like painting or poetry, he'd dismissed it. He was judging the shape of his gift instead of the power of it. And that's where most people get stuck.

They assume that truth has to feel dramatic, that gifts must be hard-won, that fulfillment comes only from reinvention. But more often than not, the truth is already inside you, quietly working through your hands, your habits, your instincts. You just haven't learned to see it as sacred yet. And I see this all the time. I hear people say, "I'm more than a dentist. I'm more than a banker. I'm more than my family's money." And I believe them. Most people *are* more than their title, but we've been trained not to trust what comes easily to us and to look outside of ourselves, always striving for something different instead of embracing that which is natural to us.

Shaquille O'Neal doesn't think it's special that he can dunk a basketball. He was born to be seven feet tall. But that doesn't make it less extraordinary. It just makes it *natural*. And that's the paradox of our gifts. They're usually the things we overlook because they've always been there. Dan Sullivan once said that from birth to age five the world encourages our gifts. After that it starts trying to beat them out of us, and then we work hard our entire lives just to retire and earn the freedom to return to the joy we started with. It's so backward! That's why I believe that living your truth starts with embracing your gifts *now*.

Your *unique ability* is the physical expression of the truth you were born with. For me, that gift is meaningful conversation. My truth lies in storytelling, in building teams around an idea, in directing projects that move people to feel and act. I don't waste my time wishing I could dunk a basketball like Shaq. People say, "I want to be more fulfilled." I say, "Then spend more time inside your gifts." Not someday. Not after you retire. *Now*.

That *one thing* you were born to do probably won't stop

whispering to you. And the closer you can build your life and business around that gift, the more your truth starts showing up in everything you touch. So here's the real question: What would your life look like if you stopped ignoring what comes naturally and started building *around* it instead?

THE ONLY STRATEGY THAT LASTS

If there's one thing I've learned after a life spent telling other people's stories—and living through my own—it's this: Truth isn't just a moral ideal. It's a strategy for fulfillment. It's not soft. It's not passive. It's the most radical, resilient force you've got.

Living your truth means following the breadcrumbs of your desire, even when they lead you off the expected path. It means standing by your values when the world hands you a shiny opportunity that doesn't feel quite right. It means choosing purpose over fear, again and again, especially when the stakes are high. It means respecting the gifts you were born with instead of brushing them off because they come naturally. The very thing you think is ordinary might just be the most extraordinary thing about you.

Living your truth requires sacrifice. You'll walk away from deals. You'll be misunderstood. You'll wonder if you're crazy, and other people will wonder it too. But you'll sleep at night. You'll look in the mirror and recognize the person looking back. And over time you'll build a body of work and a life that doesn't just look good from the outside but *feels* right on the inside.

For me, truth looks like story. It looks like building teams around meaning. It looks like producing something that outlives the moment. That's my lane, my purpose, and my north star.

But your truth? That's yours to claim. So ask yourself, "What am I here to say, to build, and to embody? And what would my life look like if I stopped *pretending* and started *producing* from a place of truth?"

In the end the most enduring legacy isn't crafted by what you achieve. It's carved naturally by the truth you're brave enough to live.

About Nick

From the slums of Port-au-Prince, Haiti, with special forces raiding a sex trafficking ring and freeing children, to the Virgin Galactic Space Port in Mojave with Sir Richard Branson, twenty-two-time Emmy Award–winning Director-Producer Nick Nanton has become known for telling stories that connect. Why? Because he focuses on the most fascinating subject in the world: *people.* As an award-winning songwriter, storyteller, and best-selling author, Nick has shared his message with millions of people through his documentaries, speeches, blogs, lectures, songs, and best-selling books. Nick's book *StorySelling* hit The Wall Street Journal Best-Seller List and is available on Audible as an audiobook. Nick has directed more than sixty documentaries and a sold-out Broadway Show (garnering forty-three Emmy nominations in multiple regions and twenty-two wins), including:

- *DICKIE V* (ESPN/Disney+)
- *Rudy Ruettiger: The Walk On* (Amazon Prime)
- *The Rebound* (Netflix)
- *Operation Toussaint* (Amazon Prime)

Nick has shared the stage with, coauthored books with, and made films featuring:

- Larry King
- Kathie Lee Gifford
- Hoda Kotb
- Dick Vitale
- Kenny Chesney
- Magic Johnson
- Coach Mike Krzyzewski
- Jack Nicklaus
- Tony Robbins
- Lisa Nichols
- Peter Diamandis
- And many more

Nick specializes in bringing the element of human connection to every viewer, no matter the subject. He is currently directing and hosting the series *In Case You Didn't Know* (season 1 executive produced by Larry King), featuring legends in the worlds of business, entrepreneurship, personal development, technology, and sports.

Nick's first love has always been music. He has been writing songs for more than two decades, and his songs have been aired on radio across the

United States and in Canada. He is currently ranked in the top 10 percent of songwriters in the world. His songs have been recorded by Lee Brice, Darius Rucker, RaeLynn, Joe Bryson, and many more, and have amassed more than three million streams on Spotify, Apple Music, Pandora, and SoundCloud. He received three Gold records in 2018 for his work with the global touring band A Day to Remember.

Nick has written and/or produced songs that have appeared on the following shows or in promotional commercials for:

- the Fox prime-time series *Glee, New Girl, House,* and *Hell's Kitchen*
- the MLB All-Star Game
- ABC Family's hit series *Falcon Beach*
- the CBS prime-time series *Ghost Whisperer* starring Jennifer Love Hewitt

CHAPTER 3

DISRUPTING CONVENTIONAL WISDOM

By Mary Moller

'll never forget the day I put my baby boy in a dresser drawer. They say you'll always remember the moment your life changed. For me, that was the moment, staring down at the baby who almost didn't make it and feeling fiercely determined to give him the life he deserved.

It had been a grueling pregnancy. For three relentless months I had to lie on my back tilted at a forty-five-degree angle in a hospital, my mind playing worst-case scenarios on repeat. I was fighting for my son before I even met him. And when he came, six weeks early and impossibly small, we brought him home to a dingy five-hundred-square-foot house with no nursery and no crib. As I looked down at his perfect face, I was confronted with a reality I hadn't been willing to name.

We were in poverty. Crushing, invisible, generational poverty, and if I didn't do something about it, my son would inherit nothing but shame.

I was twenty-eight years old with no degree, no road map, and no backup plan. I was raised to follow a certain path: grow up, get married, buy any kind of house, and keep your head down. Dreaming beyond that felt indulgent, unrealistic and even ungrateful. But something cracked open in me the moment Wyatt arrived. Suddenly mediocrity wasn't an option. He deserved better. And I knew deep in my bones that *I* was capable of more. That knowing became my fuel. I earned my BSW, then my MSW, and now I'm finishing my PhD. We started with nothing, but we didn't stay there, and along the way I began to see how much damage "conventional wisdom" can do. Because here's the truth: Gratitude is beautiful, but when weaponized, it becomes a prison. We're taught to "be grateful for what we have," as if that should silence every hunger for growth. But there's a difference between contentment and complacency. And if I had listened to that brand of well-meaning advice, I would have stayed stuck.

Just because a belief is popular doesn't mean it's correct. In fact, conventional wisdom is often the biggest enemy of transformation because it's designed to keep you safe. And I wasn't here for a safe life. I was here for *extraordinary*.

WORK HARD NO MATTER WHAT

Wyatt was barely a year old when I made the decision to build a career. I didn't just want a job; I wanted a purpose. I've always known I was meant to be a social worker. It's in my DNA. Eventually, I was recruited to join a prestigious Alzheimer's clinical team at a hospital. The commute was brutal, but I felt as if I had *made it*. I was hired to care for the caregivers. I worked with brilliant minds and aching hearts and learned so much. I was covering ten counties, coordinating education programs and pouring myself into every conversation, every mile, every moment. I loved being on the road to teach, but when the pandemic hit, I found myself stuck in the clinic five days a week. The rhythm changed, the demands intensified, and yet I felt the familiar push of that old belief: *Work hard. No excuses. Keep pushing.*

It wasn't until a quiet ache in my spirit gave me permission that I realized something I hadn't let myself admit before: I didn't want to work this way anymore. I didn't want to spend hours commuting every day. I didn't want to be stuck at a desk. My spirit was craving a little more autonomy than my position allowed.

I turned inward and laser-focused on completing my PhD so I could teach, write, and guide from a place of peace rather than pressure. I became an adjunct faculty at the University at Albany for ten years and eventually landed the dream job I have now as the executive director of the Albany Guardian Society. The belief I learned to shed is that you don't have to exhaust yourself to prove your worth. You don't owe your life to the grind. We are taught to glorify hard work as if suffering is a badge of honor. We're told that rest is laziness, that desire is indulgent, that dreams must come second to duty. But that's not wisdom; it's conditioning. And while hard work *can* be beautiful, noble, and necessary, it must be *conscious*. There is a difference between soul-driven work and survival-driven effort. One depletes you. The other builds you.

The truth I choose to live by now is this: Yes, I get to work, but I also get to create, discover, grow, love, *live*. I am not defined by how many hours I log or how drained I feel at the end of the day. I am defined by how aligned I am with what matters most.

Authentic success is in learning to pursue the dreams that keep tugging at your heart, even when they scare you. Because societal goals are designed to be seen. But soul-driven goals? They're *felt*. And when you say yes to them, you stop working for the life you think you're supposed to have and start *living* the life you were born for.

Don't Toot Your Own Horn

"Who am I to write a book?" That's what I thought the moment the email landed in my inbox. I was working at the hospital when a publishing company reached out and asked me to write a book that would help people who were caring for Alzheimer's patients. I was sure it was a scam. In fact, I was so convinced that it couldn't possibly be legitimate that I forwarded it to IT and asked them to investigate. After doing some research, they came back to me with their findings. It was real. And that terrified me.

I had been running caregiver support services for over a decade by then, and I knew this work inside and out. Yet somehow the idea of putting my name on a book felt audacious.

Still, I said yes. Secretly. I didn't tell anyone I was writing it, not because I wasn't proud but because I didn't yet believe I deserved it. When the box of books arrived, I found them waiting on my clinic chair on an ordinary Monday morning. I lifted the cardboard flap, and there it was—my name on the cover. My words, in print! There was no parade, no fanfare, but in that moment, something in me shifted. I did it! Not only that, but I realized I could do more. I had studied for years to be able to help people through gut-wrenching times in their lives, but that effort would be in vain if I stayed silent.

When we stay hidden, the people who need us most are robbed of the chance to be changed by our gifts. As Peggy Klaus writes in *Brag! The Art of Tooting Your Own Horn Without Blowing It*: "Bragging done right is not only necessary, it's a fundamental part of success." We've been conditioned to believe that humility is a virtue, but taken too far, it becomes a prison. It keeps us small, quiet, and disconnected from our own power. There's nothing noble about shrinking yourself so that others feel more comfortable. There's nothing humble about hiding your hard-earned accomplishments because you're afraid someone might think you're "too much." True humility isn't about denying your greatness. It's about *sharing* your gifts, not for applause but for impact.

When I saw that book—*my* book—I stopped waiting for permission. I stopped needing external validation and even stopped needing to convince my own internal voice of my worth. I realized that I *am* qualified. I *do* have something to say. And so do you.

What Will People Think?

Conventional wisdom convinces us that our value lies in other people's approval, as if fitting in is more important than feeling free. We're taught from a young age to obsess over how we're perceived, as though other people's comfort is the compass for our choices. Somewhere along the way, we swallowed the lie that being liked is more important than being real. The world conditions us to seek validation like oxygen, as if being misunderstood is something to fear rather than a sign that we're living truthfully. There is a hidden cost to stepping into your truth. It's not always loud or visible, but it's real. And it's steep. When you start living differently, boldly and truthfully, it stirs the water. You become the mirror for the unspoken dreams of others. You are the one who stopped settling. You are the one who dared to want *more*. And that makes people uncomfortable.

I was raised to be kind, polite, agreeable, but as I stepped into my truth, I also had to step *out*—out of certain relationships, out of old roles, out of environments that no longer felt aligned. And that wasn't easy, especially for someone who is naturally shy! For introverts like me, change doesn't just feel scary; it can feel paralyzing. But here's what I've learned: Growth lives on the other side of discomfort. And the discomfort of being judged is far less painful than the regret of never being fully seen. People will have opinions, but approval is not the same as alignment.

The truth is, every time I honored my instincts, I grew stronger. The comments still came, and the judgments still stung, but I learned to hear them as *progress* and view them as a positive sign that I was no longer playing small. "What will people think?" is the wrong question. The better question is, "What will I lose if I keep living a life that's not my own?"

Go Hard or Go Home

We live in a world that glorifies the grind. Hustle. Grit. Push. Prove. Achieve. We hear this conventional "wisdom" everywhere: *Go hard or go home.* But what if going "hard" isn't the point? What if it's not even healthy? What if the key to real, sustainable, soul-aligned success isn't about force but about *frequency*? About what you do *consistently*?

I've spent most of my career working with people who give everything they have. Caregivers are quiet superheroes managing jobs, families, aging parents, and the thousand invisible tasks no one applauds. The "go hard" mentality, while noble, is also dangerous. Because when we only know how to give, we forget how to receive. And when we ignore our own needs, we pay for it, physically, emotionally, spiritually. Caregivers often put themselves last. They're told that selflessness is saintly, that rest is a reward you earn after everyone else has been taken care of. But that's a lie. You can't pour from an empty cup. And you can't lead a meaningful life if you've left *yourself* on the back burner. So, here's what I teach caregivers and what I've learned to teach myself: You don't have to conquer mountains. You just have to *keep walking*.

If you want to be a writer, one sentence a day eventually becomes a book. If you want to get in shape, three laps around the kitchen table before you sit down triples that day's steps. The lie is that success must be big, loud, and obvious. The truth is that success is simple. It's the quiet, behind-the-scenes commitment to yourself. It's doing the thing you promised you would even when no one else is watching. It's *authenticity in action*. So let's rewrite the rule. It's not "Go hard or go home." It's "Go steady, go genuine, and go true," because a life built on small, intentional steps is far more powerful than one built on bravado and burnout.

FROM SILENCE TO STRENGTH

One of the most defining moments of my life came in the middle of a support group I was facilitating for caregivers of Alzheimer's patients. One woman, overwhelmed and breaking, looked me in the eye and asked, "How do I not get it?" I had no answer. The disease had stolen her loved one, her energy, her joy, and in that moment, I had no answer. There was no widespread prevention education. No guidance. No hope being offered. Just resignation. That question became my quest.

I started consuming everything I could about Alzheimer's disease, memory loss, and chronic illness because I had seen too many families devastated by a disease that *to some degree* is preventable. And I realized that if I didn't speak up, if I didn't step forward, nothing would change. But stepping forward meant shedding a lifetime of conditioning.

I was raised to be seen and not heard. "You have two ears and one mouth, so listen twice as much as you speak." That was yet another bit of "wisdom" I had to deprogram from my mind. My parents were loving but old-school, and the messages were clear: Be quiet. Work hard. Be a secretary. Maybe a stewardess if you're lucky. I still carry the wisdom of listening, but now I balance it with something just as sacred—*my voice*. Because my voice matters. *Your* voice matters. I always knew I was meant to teach and serve, and every moment I choose to speak my truth, I create the possibility for someone else to do the same.

Want to find your truth? What lights you up *and* scares you at the same time? What topic makes your heart race with both excitement and nerves? *That's the thread.* Pull it. Read about it. Research it. Talk to people who've lived it. Then take one small, imperfect, brave step toward it—even if life feels too busy, even if it's hard. Ask yourself what inspires you, not just what pays you. What would you do if no one was watching? How do you want to spend your days?

Because that's what this life is about: discovering what *moves* you.

My sons are thriving, my life is full, and my work is changing lives. This is what happens when we refuse to settle. The only wisdom worth following is the kind that leads you home to yourself. Conventional wisdom says, "Good things come to those who wait." But I stopped waiting. I stopped waiting for permission, for the perfect moment, for someone to choose me. I stopped waiting and started building. I built with what I had, from where I was, scared but unwilling to settle.

Good things don't just come to those who wait. They come to those who *move*, to those who *believe*, and to those who dare to become the person their future needs them to be.

About Mary

Mary Moller, PhD, is a nationally recognized expert in aging, caregiving, and social work. With over two decades of experience supporting caregivers, older adults, and professional communities, she brings deep compassion, evidence-based insight, and a powerful commitment to improving lives. Mary continues to dedicate her work to supporting older adults and the caregivers who walk alongside them—whether they're a spouse, parent, partner, relative, or friend. These everyday heroes face complex challenges when memory loss, Alzheimer's disease, or other chronic illnesses appear, and Mary has made it her mission to guide them through the journey.

Drawing on her deep experience with both individuals and large caregiver communities, Mary offers compassionate, practical strategies to help caregivers not just cope but grow. Her workshops, talks, and discussions are filled with powerful insights, actionable tools, and encouragement for people to care for themselves as they care for an aging loved one.

Mary is the executive director of Albany Guardian Society and before that she was part of the distinguished team at Albany Med's Center of Excellence for Alzheimer's disease. Experts are dedicated to improving diagnostics and health outcomes for individuals living with cognitive impairment and their caregivers.

Mary is a graduate from the University at Albany, having completed a BSW, an MSW, and a PhD, as well as the renowned Internship in Aging Program. She continues to champion the field through education—serving as adjunct faculty at the University at Albany, further deepening her contribution to gerontology and caregiver supports.

A passionate advocate for lifelong learning, health equity, and transformational practice, Mary's work informs older adults, caregivers, professionals, students, and communities alike. Her practical, empowering approach is reflected in her popular book *Alzheimer's Through the Stages: A Caregiver's Guide*, which has guided more than twenty-five thousand readers through the challenges of caregiving with clarity and support.

Her upcoming book, *The Pro-Aging Road Map: 6 Keys to Living Longer, Better, and Happier*, expands her mission—offering proactive and practical strategies to support aging with purpose and passion. Whether leading workshops, speaking at conferences, or partnering with caregiving networks, Mary continues to drive meaningful change across the aging and caregiving landscape.

Through innovation, collaboration, and education, Mary promotes a vision of aging that is inclusive, intentional, and transformative. Her voice is a trusted resource for those caring for loved ones and for those preparing to live and age healthy and well.

You can connect with Mary at Agewellworks@gmail.com.

CHAPTER 4

WHEN TRUTH FINDS ITS VOICE

By Isah Velita

It sounded like the sky cracked open. One second I was in the middle of finals week, driving home alone beneath a dark sky, papers rustling beside me on the passenger seat. The next, there was a thunderous crack, like a rock hitting my windshield, followed by an explosion of shattering glass. I was hit by a cascade of shards pelting me and stinging me over and over.

They weren't rocks...I was being shot at.

There was minimal traffic, no witnesses. The dark road that stretched in front of me suddenly felt as if it might be the last place I ever saw. Yet my first instinct wasn't to duck or panic. My first thought? Don't let her notes fly out the window. A friend had entrusted me with handwritten study guides—her bible for the ultimate exam prep. In the middle of what could have been my final moments I was gripping those pages as though they were the only thing tethering me to life.

I kept driving, thinking if I could just get home, everything would be OK. I made it home, tapped my brother on the shoulder, and said, "Call 911. I think I've been shot." Only then—when I finally registered feeling safe—did the pain descend all at once: searing, relentless, sharp, and unyielding. At that point, I dropped to the floor, clutching my leg in agony until the ambulance arrived. The car was so riddled with bullets it was a miracle that I survived. One bullet had hit where my head had just been seconds

43

earlier. Another lodged in my thigh but luckily missed the bone and artery. I had escaped death but not by much.

That night should have broken me. In some ways it did. For a while I flinched at breaking glass. I avoided freeways. I slept with the lights on. The deepest wound, however, wasn't physical. It was invisible: a wound carved by silence, judgment, and the weight of everyone who believed I had somehow caused it. I was the victim, but I was blamed for being out late, driving alone, existing in the wrong place at the wrong time. Even in a religious community that claimed to love and forgive, there was more grace for the shooter than there was for me. Part of me believed them. I wondered if it was my fault, whether an earlier argument somehow summoned chaos, or if my inner state attracted outer harm. That's what happens when your inner and outer worlds are out of alignment—you stop trusting yourself.

But here's what I've learned since: You always know. You feel it when your boundaries are being crossed. You feel it when your soul is screaming for change, even if the world around you tell you something different. You feel it when you're out of resonance with your own life, and what's on the outside no longer matches who you are inside.

That's why living your truth isn't just a catchphrase. It's survival. It's sanity. It's sovereignty. That night in 1997 didn't teach me to be afraid. It taught me to listen more closely to myself, because when you've looked death in the eye and survived, you stop performing for the world and start honoring the voice inside you that already knows the way.

LOVE, OBEDIENCE, AND THE COST OF LEADING FROM THE INSIDE OUT

I was always the one who kept things together. As the oldest, I was a child raising children. While my parents worked, I attended parent-teacher conferences, and at times cancelled plans last minute when my parents had other obligations. I even took on

44

the role of reminding my mom about appointments, helping her stay on top of a busy schedule. Back then, I thought it was normal. Only later did I learn that my childhood was early indoctrination into a dangerous pattern: perform to valued, serve to stay safe. That pattern followed me into adulthood like a shadow. Into a dysfunctional marriage. Into motherhood. Into management.

At first, becoming one of the youngest nurse managers in my network felt like a dream come true. But reality set in fast. I walked into a system where age, appearance, and background were weaponized against me. One nurse looked me in the eye and said, "I've been a nurse longer than you've been alive." Translation: Who do you think you are to lead me? It stung, but I didn't crumble. I let my work speak. What they didn't see was the invisible résumé I carried. I had been trained in leadership roles since childhood, delegating tasks to siblings, deescalating arguments, and holding the emotional weight of an entire household. In high school, I was a Drill Team Commander in NJROTC. Structure and discipline were in my bones, and advocacy was in my blood.

I didn't lead by command but by connection. I listened. I protected. I lifted people up. I empowered nurses to think differently, to rise into their potential. Yes, some people loved that. Others resented it, because not everyone is ready to be led by someone they underestimated.

Here's what I learned: true leadership has nothing to do with seniority or titles. It has everything to do with energy. That energy shifted permanently when I deployed with the U.S. Army.

Mobilization took me out of civilian healthcare and placed me in a world of discipline, accountability, and rapid adaptability. The mission— and operational readiness—became the focus, regardless of austere conditions. This role ultimately led to a civilian assignment where I was responsible for managing four outpatient clinics, each with different specialties, challenges, and cultures. I was forced to adapt—fast. That's when something clicked.

It stopped being about my résumé, where I trained, or how long I'd been in nursing. What started to matter more was how

I treated people, how I made them feel, and how I showed up—not with a checklist—but with compassion, clarity, and strength. I returned home more confident, not because I had proven myself to anyone else, but because I had proven myself to myself.

If there's one truth I want every reader to take away, it's this: You don't have to wait to live as a leader. You don't need permission from a system, a superior, or a subordinate to walk in your truth. Whether you're the oldest sibling or a newly minted manager, the truth is that how you treat people will always matter more than what's on your résumé. Others may doubt you. They may discount you because of age, gender, background, appearance, or your path, but your lived experience has value. Your energy leads before your words do. If you lead from integrity, compassion, and alignment, you will create results that even your critics cannot ignore. In doing so, you don't just forge confidence. You reclaim the authority to define your own worth.

THE INVISIBLE INJURY

In 2023 I lost the ability to walk—not because of some catastrophic event but because I ignored every signal my body tried to send me. For months I chalked the pain up to stress and tension. I took medication just to get through the day. That's what we're trained to do, especially as soldiers. We're taught to push through, override discomfort, value grit over grace. Suck it up. Lace your boots tighter. Show no weakness. Pain is just weakness leaving the body, right?

Wrong. Pain is the body's truth, and in my case, it was screaming.

By late summer I couldn't walk. The damage I previously ignored had now taken the wheel. For over six weeks I was hospitalized. It took the help of a fellow veteran before I could transfer to short-term rehab. There, I began to walk again. Slowly. Painfully. Intentionally. In 2024 I weaned myself off medications. For a while I thought I had healed, but I hadn't truly rested. Not the kind of rest that regenerates the spirit, nor the kind that rewires your nervous system after years of over-responsibility and hypervigilance.

That's the thing about burnout and trauma; they don't just ask for rest. They eventually demand it.

By early 2025, after returning from a transformative trip, the pain returned, worse than before. The MRI this time was clear. It was a herniated disc with the potential to cause permanent nerve damage. I am already losing reflex in my right foot. Still, I hesitated—but then, life sent a sign that it was time. I recently reported for Army duty and was assigned a replacement career counselor for someone who had a family emergency. The soldier I met with had recovered successfully from the procedure I'd been avoiding. She shared her story; I finally said "yes" to healing and booked the appointment. I learned that there's a difference between training and truth. Training teaches you to endure. Truth teaches you to align. And those two things are not the same. Military culture, and honestly, much of modern society, celebrates strong people who push through. But when your spine collapses, your body shuts down, and your muscles shake—that is not failure. That's feedback. That's truth trying to get your attention the only way it knows how.

I'm still learning to accept this truth: You cannot keep violating your own boundaries and expect to live in peace. When you override your body's truth long enough, it will eventually shut you down—not to punish you but to save you. We don't get extra credit for pain. We don't earn our worth through exhaustion. We don't ascend by breaking ourselves open repeatedly. At some point, strength is not staying on your feet, it's knowing when to lay down, listen, and stop carrying the weight that isn't yours.

If your body has been whispering through fatigue, headaches, gut issues, insomnia, back pain, or anxiety—listen. That's not weakness. That's wisdom. That's your truth trying to break through the noise.

KNOW YOUR VALUE

I was never what they called a "typical nurse." My path didn't start in med-surg or the ER. I was initially a certified nurse assistant, then a psychiatric technician before entering the RN field through telehealth—first in the private sector, then into the federal system. No traditional inpatient experience. For some, that made me suspect. One nurse actually said she didn't respect my authority. Why? Because I didn't follow the trajectory they were taught to believe was right. I represented something different, new, and threatening to the old guard.

But I wasn't there to copy tradition. I was there to lead transformation.

I led from my heart. I empowered the staff, trained with patience and clarity, and advocated fiercely. Under my leadership, teams didn't just function; they thrived. It wasn't because I was the loudest or smartest, but because I saw people. I believed in them until they started believing in themselves. Still, I found myself in environments where excellence was threatening. One outpatient clinic felt like a scene out of The Devil Wears Prada. I'd walk in, people whispered, "She's here," not because they were excited, but because they were intimidated. I held a high standard. I expected people to rise, and people who'd grown comfortable with mediocrity rarely respond well to that kind of light.

At another organization, my heart-led leadership was seen as a liability. Yet when I transferred to a different location, something incredible happened. Suddenly that same leadership style and energy were celebrated! They called it inspiring. Effective. Empowering. The lesson I learned is that we must go where we are valued. Perhaps you've heard this analogy: A bottle of water costs one dollar at the gas station, four dollars at the movies, and ten dollars at the airport. Same water. Same label. Different environment. The difference isn't in the bottle, but in where the bottle is placed. If someone doesn't recognize your worth, it's not a sign that you're unworthy. It's a sign that you're in the wrong place. You're the water bottle at the airport.

Not everyone will be willing to pay your price or understand the rarity of what you bring, and that's OK. Go where your leadership is celebrated and your gifts are honored.

Your value doesn't decrease just because someone else is too small to see it. You owe it to yourself—and to the lives you're meant to impact—to stand fully in your worth and go where your light isn't just tolerated but welcomed.

LIVING YOUR TRUTH ISN'T ALWAYS SHINY

Truth doesn't always come dressed in confidence. Sometimes it shows up as burnout. As a herniated disc. As a daughter saying, "This job isn't aligned with who you are anymore."

Sometimes it looks like walking away from leadership roles you once fought to earn or realizing that the thing you're best at isn't the thing your soul came here to do. Sometimes it means telling the truth to yourself before anyone else is ready to hear it.

I've served in the Air Force, been commissioned as an Army officer, and led high-performing clinics in a federal healthcare system. Yet even with all that accomplishment there was always a whisper beneath the noise: You were meant for more. Not more grind or more accolades. More resonance. More freedom. More truth.

These days I am still serving but in a different way now. I stepped down from management, and in doing so, I stepped into myself. I created space for creativity, for voiceover classes, writing, and all the things I once called side dreams but are actually core to who I am.

Maybe one day I'll build a healing space where nurses, veterans, mothers, and mission-driven women can lay their burdens down and remember who they are again. Maybe one day I'll start a podcast that allows me to exchange experiences with others. As I slow down, I live a life I deserve—free, truthful, and cared for. As I connect with others, I connect with myself. Who knows? What I do know is this: Following the breadcrumbs of joy isn't selfish. It's sacred.

We've been taught to please others before ourselves, to serve until we collapse, to wear exhaustion as a badge of honor. But you cannot pour from a soul that's run dry. Pleasing yourself and honoring what lights you up is not a detour from service. It's the bridge to it. Because when you live from your own alignment, your overflow is what nourishes the world.

So no, truth doesn't always look shiny or heroic from the outside. Sometimes it looks like disappointing others. Sometimes it looks like starting over. But what I know for sure is that truth is never lost. It's simply waiting for you to get quiet, be honest, and come home to it.

Truth has power—it reclaims you, refines you, and reveals a version of you no longer bound by approval but compelled by purpose and passion. It's a truth that honors the essence of who you really are and the difference you're here to make.

About Isah

Isah Velita is a dedicated advocate for health-care reform, focusing on organizational systems and addressing broader US healthcare challenges. Her work is driven by a personal health journey that revealed critical flaws in traditional medical approaches, leading her to embrace holistic and functional medicine alternatives.

Isah has raised awareness of systemic issues such as the prevalence of chronic illness, the mental health crisis among healthcare professionals, and the often prohibitive costs of alternative treatments. Through successful grassroots advocacy, she has influenced policy changes and is considering establishing a nonprofit organization to support healthcare reform efforts.

Her mission is to challenge outdated healthcare models and promote innovative, patient-centered solutions that ensure better outcomes and greater accessibility for all.

CHAPTER 5

TRUTH THRESHOLDS

By Wynett Isley

I n the summer of 1970 my mother turned forty-five. And then abruptly and unexpectedly died.

My father, undone by grief, retreated to his bed. He couldn't care for us, couldn't face the world. In that single season I lost everything: my mother, my home, my childhood. I was fourteen, and I learned what most adults spend a lifetime trying to ignore—the fact that nothing is permanent. What feels safe can vanish. What seems strong can shatter without warning.

But that devastation carried a second truth: When everything falls apart, something deeper has the chance to emerge. When the ground disappears beneath your feet, you don't forget how to stand. You can remember how to rise.

In the wake of this loss, my Christian faith in a greater power sustained me through the years of emotional turmoil. I began to understand that Life wasn't punishing me. It was preparing me. The pain carried a message and a lesson.

The idea that pain could be a curriculum was foreign at first. But over time I noticed patterns. Invitations. Whispers and hints. Slowly, I began to realize that I had a choice: to live by default, letting the circumstances, situations, and conditions have control, or to live by design.

Living by design doesn't mean control of every situation. It means clarity in living life with intentionality. It means choosing who you want to become. I stopped waiting for answers and started asking better questions: What is this moment here to teach me? Who am I being invited to become because of this? I stopped being a victim in my life story. And I became its author.

A Foreigner in My Own Country

When my father withdrew, I was sent to live with my aunt in Pittsburgh. Her tiny sewing room became my bedroom, and the local junior high—where I was the White girl in a predominantly Black school—became my classroom. It was the 1970s, and racial tension hung thick in the air. I felt as if I had been exiled to a foreign country. That experience could have broken me, but instead, it broke something open. My assumptions. My comfort. My idea that my way was the only way. I began to listen to learn rather than to explain. I learned a sense of humor born of pain. My classmates carried a reality I had never known. They gave me the gift of inviting me to join the truth of their experience. I still treasure that gift.

Living as the different one in their world didn't divide us; it honed my vision. On the surface I didn't belong. And in not belonging, I found the edge of my own identity. (Thank you, Romella.) In the turmoil something within me refused to die. You could take away my mother. My home. My certainty. But not my spark.

That spark—the light that refused to die—ignited my life story. Slowly I began to understand that the world doesn't hand you a manual on how to be whole. You have to write it yourself. You have to discover that spark, protect it, and design your life to nurture it so you can grow into your true self.

A Lesson in How We Heal

When my father remarried, we moved to New Jersey with his new wife. I was still raw from loss, but my stepmother was kind and taught me powerful lessons on the importance of grace through change.

I had always been a nail-biter. My parents, in a desperate

attempt to make me stop, had once smeared hot sauce on my fingers. Their logic was simple: Pain will correct the behavior. But it didn't. I just learned to love hot sauce. That's the thing about force—it can increase the pain, but it doesn't heal the cause. One New Jersey afternoon I sat beside my stepmother at the kitchen table as she painted her nails. Without saying a word, she gently took my hand and began painting each ragged nail in the same beautiful color she had painted her own. She didn't scold me. She didn't tell me to stop biting them. She didn't say anything at all. In that silent offering something inside me softened. Her simple gesture rewired something in me. I learned that change can be encouraged through tenderness. That we can be loved into transformation, no painful force required.

True healing doesn't happen when we punish ourselves into submission. It happens when we offer ourselves grace. Our culture glorifies power, control and force. We're taught to fix ourselves through sheer willpower. We fight against our own behavior. What if the reason we resist change is that it's so often presented as shame, blame, and punishment? Would we stop resisting growth if it didn't feel like a battle?

In our culture we associate growth with suffering, as if we could suffer our way into self-improvement. I've learned that pain isn't the only teacher. Grace can be just as powerful. Maybe more so. The truth is, we don't heal by hating ourselves into better behavior. We heal when we feel safe enough to choose something better. Too many times we try to shame ourselves into better habits, calling it "tough love," when really it's just bullying. Somewhere along the way we started believing that change requires harshness. That the only way to grow is to grind. But what if true transformation doesn't come from force but from compassion?

Choose True Alignment

After high school I joined the Navy like my father and my brother. I enjoyed the privilege of a successful career serving our nation as a healthcare executive and strategist. I earned a world-class education, and the opportunity to work with local, national, and international initiatives to support the improvement of the health and well-being of communities around the world.

I began working in performance improvement, helping good people grow into greatness. With strong analytical skills and my life lesson of paying attention, I began noticing that when someone talked about what they *loved*, they lit up and I noticed that spark. That spark? It's the signal, the sign pointing the way to their true self.

Most of us live from default, fulfilling expectations or failing through circumstances. But inside each of us is a divine compass. A signal system. It reveals itself through our longings and our discontent. In my work I began asking simple but life-changing questions: "What would you *love*?" not "What should you do?" or "What can you tolerate?" but "What would make you come alive?"

It's not about abandoning responsibility. It's about realigning with your truth. As a coach and consultant, I continue to be astonished and amazed by the joy of helping people and organizations discover and grow into their truth. I have an overflowing tool kit of techniques and tactics for discovery and design, and overcoming obstacles through proven, scientific systems of support. It's physics and physiology aligning people with their values, purpose, and passions. Studies in neuroscience show that purposeful work activates the brain's reward circuitry, releasing dopamine and oxytocin, chemicals that enhance motivation, creativity, and resilience.

And it doesn't stop at the individual. Teams led by people working in alignment experience less turnover, higher engagement, and better collaboration. Organizations thrive when their people are lit up!

That's why I believe alignment is a strategic priority, not just for personal fulfillment but for institutional excellence. When people are doing what they're built for, everyone wins.

THRESHOLDS AND INVITATIONS

There are moments in life that don't just change you but split your life in two: *before* and *after.* Illness. Death. Accidents. Job loss. Divorce. Empty nest. These aren't just moments; they are thresholds. Quiet ruptures in the rhythm of your life that invite you to cross over into something deeper, more honest, more *you.* But here's what most people miss: Thresholds don't always announce themselves with fireworks. Sometimes they arrive as a whisper of restlessness, a slow discontent, a subtle ache that says, "I can't keep doing this." And that ache? It isn't weakness. It's your truth trying to get your attention.

Thresholds often begin with endings. They are the moment your old identity no longer fits. They are the pause before the pivot. The disruption you never saw coming. You might feel as if your life is unraveling, but you're actually *being recalibrated* to a more aligned version of yourself.

I've spent decades studying systems, performance, and leadership. But what I've really been studying is human relations. Why people stay stuck. Why we shrink. Why we ignore the nudge to grow. The answer is always the same: fear of what stepping over that threshold might cost. But the greater cost is staying where you no longer belong. Thresholds are not detours or punishments. They are invitations to transformation. They show up to move you not to something easier but to something truer. To recognize a threshold, pay attention to your inner landscape. Do you feel something is ending, even if nothing dramatic has happened? Do you sense a quiet but growing nudge to choose differently? Do you feel called to change but unsure what that change looks like?

These are signs, and every threshold comes with its own invitation to let go of what no longer serves you, to cross into the version of you that's been waiting to emerge. Your purpose is not something you need to go find. It's already within you, beneath the noise, beneath the shoulds, beyond the fear. Thresholds are how you return to it. And the question every threshold asks is the same: Are you willing to cross the line between who you've been up until now and step into who you were born to become?

REFLECTIONS AND REDIRECTION

My oldest sister used to believe her life didn't amount to much. She believed she had drifted from one thing to the next, never settling, never achieving the kind of steady success she thought she should. She looked at my life and saw order. A thirty-six-year Navy career. Stability. Structure. Milestones and success you could measure (and spend). She thought that meant I had lived better. But I saw something different in her life. I saw texture. Depth. Adventure. I saw a soul who said yes to life, even when it didn't follow a straight line.

One day I sat with her and began reflecting her own life back to her. "Remember when you worked for that senator? Tell me about when you were in airline customer service on 9/11. Remember when you worked for FEMA? Tell me about when you were a volunteer at the Kennedy Center. Remember traveling across North America doing audits for that beauty supply company? Tell me about your adventures when you served in the Peace Corps." I pulled from her history all the twists and turns and experiences she had lived and told her I wanted to create children's books—*Adventures with Aunt Annie*—so the world could see her life the way I saw it: as rich, bold, and uniquely meaningful. She had never been taught to recognize the thread. She thought it was all chaos. I saw a beautiful arc. The thread wasn't missing; it was just tangled in the noise of comparison and expectation.

And then, she was stricken with pancreatic cancer. She passed away before we could finish those stories but not before something important happened. Thanks to our conversation, she finally saw her life as meaningful. That moment was a threshold for *me*. The invitation wasn't just to grieve. It was to remember my own gift. To write again. To hold up the mirror for others as I had for my beloved sister, because that's what truth does. It doesn't always announce itself in a big voice. Sometimes it shows up quietly through someone else's story and through the ache of unfinished dreams.

We think our lives only matter if they look impressive on paper. But our souls don't keep résumés. They keep meaning, impact, and presence. Your life may not look linear. It might feel chaotic, piecemeal, imperfect. But there is a thread. And if you can't see it yet, let someone hold up the mirror. Let someone remind you of who you've always been beneath the noise, beyond the shoulds.

My hope is that in reading this, you've recognized parts of yourself. Maybe you saw your own burnout in the staff whose gifts were misplaced and misunderstood. Maybe you saw your own doubt in my sister's voice as she wondered whether her life had meant anything at all, only to realize in the end that it had meant *everything*. Or maybe you're standing at your own threshold right now, unsure whether to stay the same or cross into something new. If so, let me say this clearly: You do not need to earn your belonging. You earned your worth at birth. You do not need to justify your desires. You grow through what you go through. The only requirement is *willingness*. Willingness to listen, to remember, and to say *yes* to the voice within that's been whispering all along. You owe it to yourself to realign with your truth and design the life you long for and live it into being. Not through force but through reverent attention, radical self-trust, and responsible compassion.

The poet Mary Oliver wrote instructions for living that have become my mantra:

Pay attention.
Be astonished.
Tell about it.

This is me telling about it, not because I have all the answers but because I've learned to pay attention, and I've helped thousands of people reflect and pay attention to their longing and discontent. I've helped individuals and institutions design a life they love living with meaning, purpose, and success.

So here is my final invitation to you: Pay attention and be

astonished. Live life with intentionality. Acknowledge the threshold moments. Trust your truth. Remember who you are. And then share your story to help others learn the truth. If you're waiting for proof that your desires matter, let this be it. This is your threshold. The moment before the becoming. You can ignore it, or you can cross it. It will bring change. It may bring upheaval. But it will also bring truth, wholeness, and the relief of knowing that you've finally acknowledged the truth and begun to live a life you love. Cross this threshold into your truth.

About Wynett

For more than twenty years Wynett "Wyn" Isley has helped leaders and high achievers grow from good to great using proven systems of success. An author, a performance improvement coach, a trainer, a speaker, a life mastery consultant, and a professional facilitator, Wyn brings a wealth of experience serving a wide variety of industries to her elite clientele of senior executives, top performers, and dedicated self-development practitioners.

Her areas of expertise include leadership development, team collaboration, performance improvement, strategic management, employee engagement, and individual personal and professional development. Wyn has two master's degrees, a graduate certificate in national strategic studies, and numerous certificates in coaching, consulting, and performance management. A decorated military retiree, she is committed to supporting those who have served the nation. She has served as adjunct faculty for several graduate schools, and she holds membership in several professional associations.

With discretion and rigorous compassion, Wyn has served clients as diverse as multibillion-dollar global enterprises, not-for-profit organizations, and veterans groups, as well as sincere individuals who want to (re)discover their dream, and learn the technology that supports them in designing and living a life they love, achieving greater success in their personal and professional lives.

Wyn is passionate about helping people succeed while becoming the best version of themselves as they discover their true selves. When she's not helping individuals and groups, Wyn enjoys quiet times in natural settings, whether in her garden in Maryland or the beautiful Smoky Mountains of East Tennessee.

Visit her website at https://wyn.coachesconsole.com.

CHAPTER 6

PRETTIER WHEN I SPEAK

By Elizabeth Aguilera

"**C**alladita te ves más bonita."

There's a beautiful rhythm to that Hispanic phrase—until you find out what it translates to: "You look prettier when you're quiet."

It was a phrase I regularly heard as a child, and I believed it. My parents emigrated from Cuba, a place of vibrant color and culture, but also a place where women were expected to smile sweetly, serve quietly, and have no aspirations beyond raising children and cooking dinner. My parents were wealthy in Cuba and enjoyed a nice life until Communism swept through like a thief in the night and they were forced to flee.

By the time I was born, the trauma of that journey had wrapped itself around my mother, and though she didn't talk about it much, her soul was heavy. She lived her life as if she were waiting for permission. She was quiet most of the day, emotionally unavailable, and spent a lot of time lying in bed and listening to the radio. It was only when my father came home from work that she would come to life, as though her existence only mattered when he walked into the room. He was a loving man, and she lived to keep him happy. That was the script she followed and the one she tried to hand to me.

My questions and needs were often dismissed, so eventually I just went quiet. I learned that challenging the status quo upset the energy of the house. I learned that the only opinion that mattered was my father's. And unfortunately, I learned to quiet the voice of my intuition, so much so that when I met the man who would become my husband, I ignored the tug in my gut that said, "Something's not right."

I was sixteen years old and thrilled to be chosen. That's how ego speaks: Be pretty. Be quiet. Be wanted. I knew it would end in disaster. I knew we were wrong for each other. I should have spoken up. But, I look prettier when I'm quiet.

THE TRUTH WHISPERS

Truth doesn't always arrive the way we expect. It doesn't come with neon signs or sudden bolts of jarring clarity. Sometimes truth comes gently, like a breeze that changes direction. That's how it came to me.

My marriage was a soul-crushing existence ripe with drama and pain. I kept hoping someone would step in and say, "This isn't right. Let me help you." But no one did. And in time I realized—they couldn't. That kind of rescue had to come from within.

It was the Fourth of July when I finally sunk into the realization that I was ready to leave. The sky above me erupted in bursts of red, white, and gold. I remember looking up at the dark sky as it lit up with color and feeling a stillness settle into my chest. And I knew. There was no fight. No shouting. No fanfare. Just a sense of peace that had eluded me for so long I almost didn't recognize it.

That night was the beginning of something sacred—a quiet revolution in my soul. Living your truth isn't always loud. Sometimes it's the decision to finally listen to the voice within that has been whispering all along and honoring what your soul has known for years. So I left. I chose myself, not out of anger but out of reverence for the life I hadn't yet lived.

What I know now is that choosing your truth isn't a one-time act. It's an ongoing practice of devotion. Life will keep offering moments that test our resolve and invite us to decide if we will abandon ourselves or stand in our truths. And each time, we are given the sacred chance to choose ourselves all over again.

WHEN LOGIC BECOMES A CAGE

I had no idea the life I so carefully built would become a blueprint for burnout. I was following the formula: get good grades, go to college, pick a major that promises security. And in the 1980s that meant computers. Computer science seemed like the sure thing, and so I grabbed it.

For years I pushed through a career that never fit, wearing the mask of competence while my spirit slowly dimmed. There was no joy, no passion, just performance. The deeper I went, the more I felt like an imposter. I became fluent in the language of sacrifice, believing that if I gave enough, achieved enough, endured enough, maybe then it would all be worth it. But what I called stability was really captivity. The golden handcuffs looked like achievement but felt like chains. I told myself I was lucky to have benefits, a salary, and a respectable job, but the cost was steep: my physical health, my mental clarity, my peace. I lived in a cycle of burnout so relentless that I had to develop a survival strategy just to make it through the week. That strategy was to retreat!

I got on a plane to Jamaica, and in that space, away from the noise, I began to return to myself. I laughed with strangers. I ate real food, moved my body, and drank water. I danced. I healed. I was unknowingly pouring life back into parts of myself I had long abandoned.

And then my entire world shifted. When I returned home, I found out that my job had been sent overseas. I had left one world behind and returned to find another collapsing. I stood in that moment gutted, not just by the loss of work but by the realization that thirty years of loyalty could be erased in an instant. I had been faithful to a system that had no intention of being faithful to me. I went into panic mode and polished up my résumé. I pushed, applied, and interviewed, desperately trying to resurrect a career I never really wanted in the first place. But this time nothing worked. The phone wasn't ringing, and deep down I knew why.

My soul was done pretending. The truth was, I didn't want to be in that world anymore. I didn't want the title, the meetings, the metrics. I wanted peace. I wanted purpose. But saying that out loud meant confronting everything I thought defined me.

We can ignore our truth for years, burying it beneath busyness, people-pleasing, or the illusion of safety. But truth waits. And when it's been silent for too long, it stops whispering and starts screaming. It throws a wrench into the life we've carefully constructed. Maybe it's a sudden breakdown, a betrayal, a burnout, or a job loss you never saw coming. The mission of our truth is to force us to face what we've tried hard to avoid, to shake the ground beneath our feet so we have no choice but to listen.

WHEN TRUTH LOOKS NOTHING LIKE SUCCESS

When I finally surrendered, I took time to think about what would feel meaningful to me. I decided to open a business serving seniors and busy moms. I cooked meals, organized homes, and provided care and companionship. It wasn't glamorous. It wasn't high paying. In fact, it was a huge step backward in income and yet a massive step forward in purpose. It felt good. It felt like me.

I didn't have a plan or a long-term vision and had no experience running a business. I simply longed to be of service. I posted an ad on Care.com, and within weeks I went from zero to fully booked. *Overbooked*, actually. Word spread, and suddenly I was being seen in a new light, not as a title or a role but as a human being who made a difference. One client said to me, "I cried every day before you came." Another said, "You gave me back my creativity." These weren't performance reviews. They were soul confirmations.

After decades in corporate life, where glowing annual evaluations left me numb, these words moved me to tears because they came from people whose lives I touched just by showing up in my truth. Still, I wrestled. The voices of doubt and skepticism crept in both from myself and concerned friends. "This isn't a real job," I heard. "What will people think?" But every time I tried to talk myself out of it, my heart pulled me closer in.

The truth is, your path may not make sense to anyone else. It may look like a step down when, in fact, it's a return to grace. People couldn't always see what I saw. They saw the title I gave up and the salary I walked away from. That's the thing about living your truth—it's not always understood by the people you love the most. It challenges their expectations, breaks invisible contracts, and disrupts what they've grown accustomed to. But it brings you home to yourself.

Living your truth is a daily practice, not a destination. It is both beautiful and brutal. You will battle doubt, face judgment, and question yourself a thousand times. But if you stay the course and hold fast to the quiet, pulsing *yes* inside you, you'll discover something extraordinary: Your truth doesn't just free you. It makes you the kind of person who sets others free.

THE TRUTH IS FLUID

After six years had passed, I could feel a change was coming. You see, our truth isn't stagnant. It expands with us. It evolves as we do. And just when we think we've found "it," something deeper begins to call. I didn't have all the answers. I only knew there was more I was meant to give. More I was meant to become. That's when coaching found me. Not everyone understood. "Wouldn't it be easier to just go back to a steady job?" they asked. So I stopped trying to explain.

I withdrew and kept to myself, not in bitterness but in reverence for my own path. I no longer felt the need to convince anyone of what I was doing or why. I just did the work. Quietly. Consistently. Every single day. I stayed the course, and eventually I found my mission: helping women and men become emotionally bulletproof after narcissistic abuse. But even that truth didn't come in a flash. I tried on three different "ideal clients." Each time nothing fit—until I looked in the mirror. The client I'd been searching for was me. The ideal avatar was me! I had resisted it. I didn't want to go back to the pain I'd worked so hard to overcome. But the truth kept nudging me, and eventually I gave in!

Over the past year or so, I've built a program and launched it into the world, and while it's not yet bringing in millions, it's a soul-level success. This is the messy middle where truth clarifies, courage builds, and our destiny unfolds piece by piece. It's also usually the space in which people give up. It's easy to dismiss our endeavors as failures if we don't see an immediate ROI, but that's a mistake. You see, we are in relationship with our truth. And relationships take time, patience, and love.

Truth, like any relationship, deepens with devotion. And the more I chose to show up for it, the more it revealed who I was meant to be, how I was meant to serve, and the gifts that are on the other side of surrender.

THE SACRED WORK OF KNOWING YOURSELF

"Make it work." For a long time that was my mantra, and to be fair, there's something admirable about that kind of grit. It speaks of loyalty, resilience, and strength. But strength, when misdirected, can quickly morph into self-betrayal.

I stayed in a marriage that was breaking my heart. I stayed in a job that drained the life out of me. I told myself I was committed, but really, I was disconnected from myself. It's not strength to stay where you are slowly disappearing. It's not loyalty to keep investing in something that gives you nothing in return. And it's not noble to sacrifice yourself on the altar of "making it work."

The truth is, you can't know what's worth fighting for until you know *yourself*. You have to know your values and what you stand for. You have to get clear on your standards, your boundaries, your sacred *no*. You need to understand your rhythms, your desires, and your worth *independent* of what the world reflects back to you.

Ask yourself:

- What am I tolerating that's costing me my peace?
- Where have I been trying to "make it work" out of fear rather than alignment?

- What have I been pretending not to know about what I need?
- Who am I when no one is watching and I'm not performing for approval?

Without that inner clarity, you're vulnerable to every opinion, every expectation, every narrative that says, "This is who you should be and what you should want." But once you know, you move differently. You speak with conviction. You walk away when something violates your truth, not because you're angry but because you're anchored.

Knowing yourself gives you the eyes to see clearly, the voice to speak bravely, and the strength to walk away when your truth whispers, "It's time."

This journey has changed me in ways I couldn't have imagined. The woman I am today bears almost no resemblance to the woman I was when I left corporate life. That version of me was terrified. Terrified of making the wrong move. Terrified of being judged. Terrified of disappointing others, of not being able to keep it all together, of stepping outside the lines and falling apart.

She lived in fear and called it responsibility. She silenced herself and called it humility. She settled and called it success. But now I know better. I am no longer trying to hold it together for the sake of appearances. I've watched the things I clung to fall away— my security, certainty, and savings—and I'm still here. I've made mistakes, disappointed people, and pivoted more times than I can count. And yet I didn't break. I *became*. I always had a voice, but I didn't use it. I always had power, but I didn't know it. Now I do. I've gone from fearing change to welcoming it as a companion, not a threat. I've learned the real prizes aren't in the titles, paychecks, and applause. The prize is in who you become as you tune in to what your heart really needs in order to thrive.

They told me I was prettier when I was quiet, but truth has made me luminous in ways silence never could. And I'm not here to look pretty. I'm here to feel *alive*!

About Elizabeth

Elizabeth Aguilera is a narcissistic abuse recovery coach, speaker, and advocate for survivors of emotional and psychological abuse. After spending thirty years in corporate IT, Elizabeth's career was suddenly uprooted when her job was sent overseas. That turning point led her to create a heart-centered business helping seniors and overwhelmed moms—a natural extension of her deep compassion and desire to serve.

Today, Elizabeth draws from her own healing journey, professional training, and decades of life experience to support women and men in loosening the grip of the trauma bond and reclaiming their inner strength. She is passionate about helping others rebuild unshakable self-trust, something she calls becoming *emotionally bulletproof.* Her transformational eight-week program, *It's Not Your Fault!,* is the guide she wishes she had during her own recovery—a powerful and compassionate road map for healing, setting boundaries, and finally feeling free.

Elizabeth is a certified life coach through the Brave Thinking Institute and a member of the International Coaching Federation. She has been surrounded by a close-knit circle of friends for over forty years and believes in the power of deep, lasting connection. When she's not coaching or writing, you can find her singing in her church choir, cooking for friends, or curled up with a good book and her grand-cat, Daisy, purring happily beside her.

Learn more:

- thegoodcalling.com
- itisnotyourfault.carrd.co
- linkedin.com/in/elizabethaguilera
- youtube.com/@ElizabethAguileraCoach

CHAPTER 7

THE PLATFORM

*How I Chose Legacy Over Fame and
Built a Life That Can't Be Ignored*

By Sir Michael Fomkin

The kitchen was hot, loud, and unforgiving. Steam rose from the sinks like smoke, clouding the air. I stood in a three-foot strip of wet tile, my hands burning raw from hours of scrubbing trays.

I was fourteen. A Brooklyn kid raised by a single mom who worked twice as hard for half as much. The streets I came from didn't hand out opportunities; they handed out lessons—the kind you either learn quickly or pay for slowly. And somewhere in the back of that kitchen I was learning something school couldn't teach: No one was coming to save me. If I wanted more, I'd have to become the *source* of more.

At the time, I didn't know any of that. What I couldn't see yet was that those moments were *preparation*. They were forming something in me that I would spend the next three decades uncovering: The ability to turn obscurity into opportunity, struggle into structure and silence into a stage.

If I could go back and tell that kid one sentence of truth, it would be this: "You're not here to scrub dishes. You're here to change lives." Years later I would come to understand that you don't wait to be discovered. You don't hope someone gives you permission to lead. You *become* the platform. You *build* the stage. You *create* the room people want to be in, and then you *invite others* to shine beside you.

This isn't a chapter about chasing fame. It's about choosing legacy. It's about understanding that every minute matters, that who you surround yourself with shapes your future and that success isn't a spotlight, but a signal you send by the way you show up. And that signal? It started with a kid in a kitchen who decided not to wait for the world to recognize him, but instead, become impossible to ignore.

THE PLATFORM BUILT ON FALSE FOUNDATIONS

I was twenty-one years old, standing in a corner showcase on Madison Avenue, dressed like a man twice my age and commanding a thirty-million-dollar book of business as the youngest manager in the history of Tourneau Watches. I was a rising star, shaking hands with hedge fund titans, celebrities, and CEOs, selling watches that cost more than cars. People looked at me and saw success. What they didn't see was what I saw one night, locking up the store.

I glanced at my reflection in the thick glass door, tailored suit, polished shoes, Rolex on my wrist. And all I could think was, "Is this really it?" It was a gut punch. I wasn't leading. I was *performing*. I'd mastered the art of selling but was starving for purpose. I saw the blueprint I'd been living: Rise quickly, earn respect, dress well, close the deal. But I was building someone else's dream, and I couldn't do it anymore.

There's a moment in everyone's life when the outer world no longer matches the inner world and something has to give. I walked away from the prestige, not out of recklessness, but out of *reverence* for something more. A bigger vision. A deeper calling. At some point along the way, I had lost my values and myself. I remember talking to my friend Tony Robbins and he asked me a powerful question. "What's the price you're paying for being out of alignment?"

That question tore through every illusion I had, because the cost of pretending is steep. I went back to the foundation, and brick by brick, began building something different. Not a storefront.

A platform. A message. A *movement*. That's the fire that lit *VIP Ignite*. Not fame or followers, but *freedom*…the kind that comes from living your truth.

IGNITE FROM THE INSIDE OUT

Walking away from the luxury world didn't mean I had a plan, but I had something better: *a pull I couldn't ignore.* That's what led to the creation of *VIP Ignite*. I knew there were people out there like me who had a voice, but no platform; people with talent, but no access. They were people waiting to be discovered, when what they really needed was the power to *ignite themselves.* So that's what I built—a launchpad! *VIP Ignite Live* became the place where untapped potential meets undeniable visibility and ordinary people finally get the platform they need to be seen.

Most entrepreneurs don't fail because they lack strategy. They fail because they're chasing the wrong things and listening to the wrong people. They fall victim to shiny object syndrome, buying into hype instead of investing in *alignment.* That's the difference that saved me. I didn't just surround myself with people who were "famous." I aligned with people who had already walked the path I was on. Tony Robbins. Jack Canfield. Joe Vitale. Brian Tracy. Not just mentors. *Mirrors.* They reminded me that proximity is power and that success isn't about being seen, it's about *providing value to others.*

The light you surround yourself with becomes the reflection you cast. That's the secret. You don't wait to be invited. You build the room people want to be in. You *become the source* of opportunity. That's why I bought The Miami News. After winning five Pulitzer Prizes, the paper had been shelved. It was put up for sale for $18 million, and when no buyer came, Cox Communications let it die. Print was fading but I saw a stage. So, I acquired it and relaunched it on a fully digital platform. I didn't just want another media brand; I wanted a global spotlight I could use to lift others up. Now, *The Miami News* gives me access; press passes to the

White House, backstage access at major events and a stage people want to be on. That's influence—when you are the platform, you have something to offer and you *become the one they can't ignore.*

THE MAN ON THE MOON

I was five years old when my dad died. Before he passed, he gave me a folded newspaper. It was the edition that captured the day Neil Armstrong walked on the moon. That paper lived in our house for years, and I clung to it like a compass.

Fast forward decades later, I was starting my career and hosting a radio show when a press release came across the wire: a gala was being held at Ohio State University in honor of astronaut John Glenn. I knew in my gut I *had* to be there. Not for business. For my dad. We had just launched the company and had no money, but I grabbed my partner and drove ten hours through a blizzard from New York to Ohio. The press conference was over in five minutes, and we didn't even get a photo. But I wasn't giving up. We asked if we could meet him and were told we could take a quick picture with Glenn at a student luncheon—no interview, just a handshake.

That's when fate took over.

My partner struck up a conversation in the restroom with a woman who turned out to be Annie Glenn, John's wife. As we were talking to her, John Glenn himself walked over and Annie said, "John, I want you to meet my dear friends Michael and Alycia. They'll be joining us for lunch." Just like that, we were in. Lunch turned into an invitation to a black-tie dinner honoring the Gemini program. I was standing mesmerized, taking it all in, when the doors swung open. A full military brigade entered, and the room went silent. They walked to our table and John Glenn stood and said, "Michael, meet my dearest friend, Dr. Neil Armstrong." I shook hands with the first man to walk on the moon. I sat down to dinner with a childhood hero and I realized something that changed my life forever: Your dreams live in you, waiting for the moment you're bold enough to chase them. I wasn't invited. I didn't have credentials or money. I *had a reason*. A memory. A *why*. And I *moved* on it.

Let this be the reminder, you are already enough to *belong*, but you have to put yourself in the rooms where your future is waiting. I didn't just meet Neil Armstrong. I fulfilled a promise to my dad. That's the power of presence and of saying yes, even when the world tells you no.

If you want to be in the room, get in the room. If you want to be a writer, then write! The moment you take action, you *are* one. If acting is your goal, stop saying, "I want to be an actor," and instead say, "I *am* an actor." The title isn't given; it is *claimed*. And the fastest way to get there is to decide you're there already.

A Sword, a Standard, and a Story Worth Living

When I was a kid, I was fascinated with knights. They *stood for something*. Honor. Valor.

I had no idea that one day I'd be knighted by the oldest royal knighthood in the world. It started when I met Bill Walsh of Powerteam International. Bill had helped build nine-figure companies, traveled by private jet, and had access to rooms most people would never enter. What impressed me most wasn't his success, but his *wisdom*.

When someone like that talks, you listen. That's what set me apart. I listened, followed through and showed up for him whenever he needed me. That kind of loyalty leaves an impression. He told the person in charge of the knighthood, "In fifty years of business, Michael is the only person who actually listened to what I said and *implemented it*." That led to an invitation to be knighted by the Royal House of Cappadocia, the oldest knighthood in existence. You can't *buy* a knighthood. You have to be *recommended*. And not for what you've built, but for how you serve. My team and I are committed to service. In every city visit, we donate twenty-five thousand meals to needy families. We've helped rescue over thirty-five hundred people from sex trafficking, and we are currently raising twenty million dollars to build schools around the world. *Real success gives back.*

I learned that from my mother. She raised me alone, worked hard and eventually got her PhD. She'd make one-of-a-kind meals throwing all the leftovers together not because it was trendy, but because that's all we had. I never knew we were struggling because she wrapped sacrifice in dignity.

When I received the sword and was asked what I wanted engraved, I didn't put my name. I asked for the names of my father and grandfather. That sword was a commitment to *build something better for the next generation.* Because a platform means nothing if it ends with you. Success is not about how high you rise, but about how many other people rise because you lived.

THE PLATFORM MUST BE TESTED

You don't think about your expiration date until life dares you to. In 2024 my dare came like a sucker punch. I was *finally* getting healthy. My mom had passed the year before, and the grief cracked open a new awareness that time doesn't stretch forever. I decided to get serious about my health and got advanced labs done. I wanted to lose weight, eat clean, and move better. But the bloodwork came back off. My thyroid wasn't functioning right, and they found a nodule that looked potentially cancerous.

I was doing everything *right,* and now I was staring down one of the darkest tunnels of my life. The doctors told me to wait six months. *Watch and see.* But I wasn't built for passivity. I'd spent my whole life raising my standards. I wasn't about to lower them now. I found the best thyroid surgeon in the world and called her. I had the procedure within a week and thank God I did. It *was* cancer. They got it, but had I sat back and taken the advice to wait, I might not be here writing this chapter. That was the day everything changed. Not because I beat cancer, but because I saw, for the first time, how fragile this entire platform could be. I hadn't updated my legacy documents. I hadn't set up a trust or made plans for what happens to the business if I'm not around to lead it. I was so busy *building* the fire, I forgot to ask if it could burn without me.

So I cleaned up the systems and got clear on succession. I tightened up my circle, cut out distractions, and recommitted to my *why*. I went deeper with God and my family. I stopped wasting minutes on Netflix scrolls and started squeezing the juice out of every moment. Because *minutes become days—and days become legacy.*

Today, I'm the healthiest I've ever been and here's the truth: Most people say they want more—but they wait. They wait to get in shape, to chase the dream, to write the book, step on the stage, start the thing they can't stop thinking about. They wait... until the time runs out. But if this is the life you want—*be it*. Not someday. *Today.*

You don't become a writer by dreaming of books. You become a writer by sitting down and writing. You don't become an actor by wishing for roles. You become an actor by *showing up as one—* right now. Wake up one hour earlier. Go to bed one hour later. That's two hours a day. Do the math, and that's *twelve extra weeks a year*. Twelve extra weeks to build your dream, to invest in your family, to become who you're meant to be.

Today we're standing at the edge of a new era—one where machines can outthink us. The Industrial Age rewarded labor. The Information Age rewarded knowledge. But this era belongs to *connection*, humanity, and those bold enough to bring heart back into the equation. While job markets evolve, *purpose never goes out of style*. AI can't replicate you, your tone, your touch, your timing. It can't replace your empathy, your vision, your truth. And that's your greatest edge.

So how do you stand out now? You become the platform. You build the room others want to be in. You create value through relationships, impact through experience, and legacy through alignment. That's how billion-dollar empires were built before the internet. And that's how *you* build a life that matters.

Because after the accolades, the headlines, the pivots and the pain, what matters most is that you stayed the course. That you dared to live in resonance with your truth. That you showed up when it was hard and kept going when it didn't make sense. That you didn't wait to be chosen...you *chose yourself.*

And because you did, lives were changed, dreams were launched, and a legacy was born that will echo far beyond your lifetime.

About Michael

For over two decades, Sir Michael Fomkin has been a pioneering force in the entertainment, business, and personal development industries. As the founder of VIP Ignite, Truth Mgmt, and Vision-Craft, Michael has helped launch the careers of thousands of aspiring actors, models, and entrepreneurs—empowering them to break into some of the most competitive industries in the world.

Michael is a number-one best-selling author, having coauthored books with legendary business minds such as Michael Gerber, Brian Tracy, and Dr. Joe Vitale. His groundbreaking work in branding, storytelling, and personal positioning has been featured in *Forbes* and *Entrepreneur*, and on ABC, CBS, and Fox News.

As a knighted philanthropist, Sir Michael has set a goal of raising twenty million dollars to build schools in Kenya, supported the rescue of over thirty-five hundred children from sex trafficking and continues to champion causes that blend purpose with power. His visionary leadership has generated over $150 million in sales through live and virtual events. His clients have gone on to star in major ad campaigns, walk runways at Fashion Week, and appear in blockbuster films and television series.

Most recently, Michael cocreated CAST-GPT™, the world's first AI-powered casting assistant for models and actors—revolutionizing the way talent is discovered and represented. He is also the founder of Legends Circle, an elite mastermind for high-performing entrepreneurs seeking mentorship from iconic industry leaders.

When he's not creating new platforms, mentoring talent, or sharing the stage with the world's most influential minds, Michael enjoys spending time with his family, exploring history, and honoring his heritage in Brooklyn, New York.

Learn more:

- vipignitelive.com
- truthmgmt.com
- visioncraftlive.com

CHAPTER 8

WHY HONESTY ISN'T JUST A VIRTUE—IT'S A SURVIVAL MECHANISM

By Ryan Reichert

A ccording to the Bible, there are seven deadly sins—and I've committed them all.

But it was lust that finally unraveled my life. I was standing in the garage, on the phone with a woman I'd met on Match.com, when my wife opened the door and asked who I was talking to. I don't know if it was bravado, surrender, or just the unbearable weight of living a lie—but I told her the truth. There was shouting, understandably. And standing in the doorway was my youngest daughter, who heard it all. The marriage was over. The next evening I went to my first AA meeting.

But if I'm telling the truth—and I have to now, for reasons you'll soon understand—my need to hide didn't start there. It started back in high school, when a knee injury led to a painkiller addiction. I recovered, grew up, and by twenty-five, I was an Airborne Ranger in Afghanistan, leading thirty-one men through hell.

I went through four combat deployments, lost too many friends and spent many sleepless nights replaying every moment I couldn't undo. I looked tough. I acted tough. But inside, a war raged that no one could see. I made it twenty-three years, and in 2019 I took one final deployment—one last push so we could finally settle down in Washington State. My best friend and I were going to open a business, and I was finally going to live a life on my own terms. But nine months into that deployment, I got the call. My wife and daughters had gone to Minnesota to visit family and decided they wanted to stay. In a single phone call the dream I'd been holding on to for years disappeared. That's when the real struggle began. Resentment. Disappointment. Grief I couldn't name, let alone share.

I retired in Minnesota and on paper, I had it all: a beautiful wife, two daughters, a home, a boat, money in the bank. But inside I was drowning in shame and loneliness.

That's one thing no one in the army prepares you for. The loneliness hits hardest when the noise stops and you're left to face yourself in the silence. So I did what I had always done when the pain got too loud. I hid behind alcohol, pills, pleasure seeking, and anything else I could find to outrun the cocktail of guilt, fear, and failure that had coursed through me.

The night my wife caught me cheating, everything shattered, but for the first time in decades I told the truth. To myself. To God. And the next day to a room full of strangers in folding chairs. And I haven't stopped since. Today I am eighteen months sober. I am a born-again Christian author and owner of Our Protector Development, a consulting firm specializing in personal, professional, and leadership development.

I've learned the hard way that survival depends on truth and that while truth is rarely convenient, it is always the right path. Living in contradiction to your truth isn't just emotionally exhausting; it's physically damaging. In fact, studies show that chronic self-betrayal and suppression of truth activate the brain's stress response, flooding the body with cortisol and adrenaline. Over time this leads to anxiety, insomnia, weakened immunity, even heart disease. When you live a lie—whether to protect others, avoid conflict, or preserve an image—your nervous system *stays* in survival mode. Truth, on the other hand, is regulation. Alignment. It's not always comfortable, but it's the only place where real peace begins.

The truth will cost you. It might cost you your comfort, your image, sometimes even your relationships. But the price of a lie is heavier. A lie demands everything and leaves you empty. The truth makes demands too, but at least it sets you free.

MANAGE THE VOICE IN YOUR HEAD

Learning to live your truth means first learning to *discern* it, because not every voice in your head is honest. Some lies sound like reason. Some fears feel like facts.

Before you can control your life, you have to control your mind. If you don't, something else will.

In 2019 I deployed to Saudi Arabia. It wasn't supposed to be a difficult tour. I was advising the National Guard, helping prepare them to defend their homeland. It was meant to be my final mission before retirement. I could see the finish line and kept my focus on the fact that it wouldn't be long before I was relaxing in Washington State, a vision I had clung to in my darkest moments. But the closer I got to freedom, the louder the noise in my mind became. The deployment turned dark fast. On September 14, 2019, a coordinated drone and missile attack struck Saudi Arabia's Abqaiq and Khurais oil facilities—key sites in the global energy supply chain. The attack revealed the vulnerability of even the most fortified infrastructure and for those of us nearby, it was a chilling wake-up call. It was becoming more and more dangerous. I couldn't sleep, so I was mixing NyQuil and melatonin just to shut my brain down. The old demons came back; faces of friends I'd lost, memories I thought I'd buried, the ache of too much grief and not enough peace. So when my wife called in the middle of it to tell me she didn't want to retire in Washington, it added lighter fluid to the fire in my mind.

When I finally returned home, I was running on adrenaline, and when the adrenaline wore off, the pain swallowed me whole. I didn't know what I was doing anymore. I didn't know who I was or where I belonged. The PTSD I had suffered after a brutal tour in Afghanistan in the early 2000s seemed to return in full force. Back then I couldn't sleep unless I'd checked every window three times, determined to keep the enemy out. Now I seemed to frantically search for an escape from the enemy within. The inner monologues that seemed to run on repeat in my mind went something like this: "You're not good enough. You'll mess it up. You don't deserve peace. You're broken. You'll never be happy." Over and over again. It wasn't until later that I understood the truth: Whatever voice you let dominate your mind will eventually dominate your life.

Bruce Lee once said, "Words have power. It's why they call it 'spelling.' Every time you speak, you're casting spells." My life had become the sum of the spells I was casting with my thoughts. Only I wasn't casting spells; I was throwing curses! Looking back, I can trace it all the way to age fourteen. After my football dreams were crushed by a knee injury, they gave me morphine and Oxycontin. That's when I learned what it meant to escape. Later it was alcohol. Then it was ambition. Then fantasy. Any time the truth got too loud, I chose numbness instead of surrender. I had built a bulletproof mask instead of a bulletproof mind. And that's the lesson.

If you want to survive change, if you want to thrive in the face of fear, you have to learn to direct the dialogue in your head. The truth will set you free. But first it will demand that you silence every lie you've ever believed about yourself, because the life you're building can only be as strong as the voice narrating it.

CHOOSE YOUR HARD

At some point you realize that life is hard either way. Marriage is hard, but divorce is hard too. Being in shape is hard. Being out of shape is hard. Telling the truth is hard. Living a lie is harder. You have to choose your hard.

For most of my life I chose the wrong hard. I chose silence over truth. Performance over peace. Other people's happiness over my own integrity. I kept trying to outrun the voice in my head instead of realizing that I had control over it. That voice got louder during my final deployment in Saudi Arabia. We were living in isolation, just five of us in a cluster of small villas during COVID, not allowed to interact. I was cut off from everything that made me feel human. I was alive, technically. But spiritually? I was gone. I was sick and tired of being sick and tired. Living seemed *hard*. Raised Catholic, I grew up believing God was vengeful. That every mistake added a black mark to some eternal tally sheet. I didn't know yet that God wasn't angry. I was. At my darkest moment, I almost chose the wrong hard—and put a gun in my mouth. Then I heard a knock at the door.

My Master Gunner stood there, asking to borrow flour and sugar. Flour and sugar. Something so simple. So human. So normal. It wasn't a vengeful God that intervened but a merciful one. That knock saved my life. You see, we are always choosing our hard. The key isn't to escape pain but rather through our pain to find purpose. Infidelity? That was hard. But so was the lie I'd been living inside my marriage. I thought I was protecting my family by pretending, but the truth is, *I was just afraid*. Afraid to say, "This isn't working." Afraid to say, "I'm not OK." Afraid to choose the honest hard over the deceptive easy. If I had spoken the truth sooner, the marriage might have still ended, but it could have ended in peace instead of destruction. The sooner you tell the truth, the sooner the healing begins.

My divorce led to my sobriety. My darkest moment led to divine presence. My spiritual bankruptcy led to a total rebuild. Pick your hard. Pick the one that aligns with truth, not fear. Pick the one that leads to freedom, not more pretending. Pick the one that might hurt now—but heals you later. Because the wrong hard will cost you your soul. The right hard will give it back.

THE POWER OF PRACTICE

There's a reason the word *ritual* is inside the word *spiritual*. Growth isn't just a moment of insight—it's a daily decision. You don't drift into truth. You commit to it. Over and over again. After my life fell apart, I started asking myself a question every day: What's the cost of not practicing truth?

For me, the answer is simple. If I don't do the work, *I go back.* Back to drugs. Back to alcohol. Back to hiding, numbing, lying. Back to the man I swore I'd never be again.

So I built a system. Now, every single day, no matter what, I make time for my practice. I list ten things I'm grateful for. Gratitude is the antidote to entitlement and despair, and it reminds me that even when I'm hurting, I'm still blessed. Still here. I pray for three people I don't like. That's right. I don't just pray for the people I love; I pray for the ones who challenge me, frustrate me, maybe even people who betrayed me. I meditate for five minutes. For me, stillness is a weapon against runaway thoughts that threaten to pull me under. And finally, I thank God for the day. It doesn't matter if it was a good day or a bad day; I thank Him, because every day that I wake up sober and honest is a miracle.

When I work with clients now, I encourage them to practice the power of threes. The idea is to get a win in each of the three main categories of life.

1. A physical win—a walk, a run, a workout—something that reminds my body it's still alive.

2. A mental win—reading, journaling, learning something that grows my mind instead of numbing it.

3. A spiritual win—a moment of presence, prayer, or peace that roots me in who I want to be.

Truth isn't a one-time confession; it's a way of life. And ritual is what keeps you on the path when motivation disappears. Ritual is what builds identity, and it's what transforms healing from a moment into a movement.

There were days, especially early on, when I didn't want to do any of it. Days I felt numb. Days I still heard the voices of shame and self-doubt. But I did it anyway. And that *anyway* is where transformation lives.

TELL THE TRUTH NO MATTER WHAT

If you've made it this far, you've seen my life laid bare. Not the polished version. The raw, roller-coaster journey that challenged me, revealed me, and ultimately set me on the path to greater purpose. It wasn't pretty, but it was real, and more importantly, it is mine. And if there's one thing I hope you take from it all, it's this: The hardest battles are never on the battlefield. They're in your mind. They're in your silence. They're in the words you're too afraid to say and the truths you're not quite ready to claim.

I've faced down death in combat and led men into war zones, but nothing has scared me more than telling the truth—about who I am, what I've done, what I want, and what I believe.

The real war was never with the enemy overseas. It was with the voice in my head. But here's what I know now: When you tell the truth, fear loses its power.

These days I still feel triggered at times, but I move forward anyway because I know now that fear isn't a stop sign. It's a signal that I'm standing at the edge of my next breakthrough. I've built a new life—one rooted in daily rituals, unshakable honesty, and the quiet courage to choose the right *hard*.

I am now committed to living a life of honesty no matter what the cost because I know that the benefits of honesty, while sometimes slow to come, far outweigh the temporary safety of deceit. I encourage you to do the same. Speak your truth. Even if your voice shakes. Even if people don't understand. Even if you're afraid. Even if it comes with consequences. Because the truth will break what needs to be broken—and will build what's meant to last.

About Ryan

Ryan T. Reichert is a born-again Christian, an author, a speaker, a podcaster, and a servant leader with over four decades of life experience, working across small-town America to global metropolises. He is a retired lieutenant colonel, serving twenty-three years in the US Army, including airborne, ranger, and multiple combat deployments. Following his military career, he transitioned into the Fortune 500 world, gaining insight into corporate leadership and strategy.

Today, Ryan is cofounder and owner of Our Protector Legendary Leadership Companies, providing one-on-one coaching, group and leadership coaching, Keynotes+Seminars+Trainings+Live Events, and book-writing support—under the Our Protector Development umbrella, featuring the book series, professional speaking, executive coaching, and media with *Our Healer, Our Protector* podcast.

Above all, Ryan's greatest passion is helping others. Whether through volunteering, advocacy, or service, he goes wherever God leads him, committed to making a lasting impact wherever he is sent. His journey as a recovering alcoholic and addict, father, and business owner continues to shape his mission—guiding others toward faith, purpose, and transformation.

Website: www.OurProtectorDevelopment.com

Podcast: Our Healer Our Protector (located on YouTube, Apple Podcast, Amazon Music, Deezer, and Spotify)

Social media: Instagram: @armyrt1978, Facebook: @RyanT.Reichert, LinkedIn: @RyanReichert78, X: @RyanTReichert, TikTok: @armyrt1978, YouTube channel: @OurHealerOurProtector

CHAPTER 9

THE COMPASS WITHIN

Critical Thinking as a Bridge to Critical Truth

By Catherine Cooper

Lhe air was thin and unforgiving at twenty thousand feet. I couldn't find the trail. It was supposed to be a quick hike from base camp—an easy detour before nightfall—but as the shadows lengthened across the Himalayas, it became terrifyingly clear: I was lost. Alone. No idea if anyone even knew I was missing. The altitude fogged my mind. I thought about hunkering down and waiting to be found. But something deeper stirred—an instinct to keep moving no matter what. I didn't know which way was the correct one, but I knew staying still would kill me. So I picked a direction and walked. Hours later, as my camera flash blinked weakly in the dark to guide my way, I saw a glint of light in the distance. A search party. Salvation.

That night taught me what no classroom ever could: Critical thinking begins not in confidence but in chaos. It's what we reach for when fear floods the brain and instinct is all we have left. It's not about always being right. It's about being willing to think when nothing is certain.

In the absence of structure, without a guide or guarantee, the mind learns to stretch. To observe more carefully. To question assumptions. To hold opposing possibilities at once. In that Himalayan dark, I wasn't just navigating a mountain; I was navigating myself. Fear wanted to shut me down. But the act of asking, "What now?" instead of, "Why me?" was the spark that kept me alive.

Critical thinking is born in these moments of rupture. It's refined in discomfort, not in ease. It's less about IQ and more about inquiry. It grows strongest when the path disappears and the only compass you have is the willingness to respond deliberately, curiously, and with courage. And perhaps most importantly, it's how we begin to find our truth, because truth doesn't arrive fully formed. It unfolds. And the ability to think critically—to separate noise from signal, emotion from meaning, conditioning from inner knowing—is the skill that helps us see it.

In that sense critical thinking is not just a mental muscle. It's a soul skill, a way of returning to what's real, especially when the world is trying to convince us otherwise.

That night, I walked out of the mountains with more than just a survival story. I walked out with a new understanding: that clarity isn't always something you start with. Sometimes it's what you earn when you dare to think through the dark.

NOT MY SCRIPT

Growing up in a mainstream middle-class family, I was handed a life plan. Go to school. Get a good job. Get married. Have kids. I didn't hate that plan; it just never felt like mine. I remember standing in line at a college dive when a friend said, "I can see you driving a station wagon, five kids in the back." He meant it as a compliment, but as I test-drove that vision, I just couldn't picture myself in that station wagon, let alone a minivan. That moment didn't just plant doubt; it unearthed a knowing. I didn't want the expected life. I wanted something wild. Unscripted. *Real*.

At twenty-four, I had my dream job in production working on sports content for a major television network. Then, as our company was tagged to produce programming for a brand-new channel, I was able to head that up, and it was adventure sports, mountains and water, my favorite things. Traveling. Succeeding. But somewhat empty. Most lunch breaks I'd venture to the cathedral next door not only to pray but to reflect and often cry. Something was misaligned. The work was exciting, but my soul wanted more.

One day I finally told myself the truth: I wanted out. I wanted to backpack the world and learn from people, not just film them. The moment I gave myself permission to want that life, I felt weightless. Telling my boss and my father was terrifying. They thought I was nuts. But deep down I knew this was my first bold step toward living my truth.

NAVIGATING STANDARDS AND BELIEFS

Fiji was my first stop. Ten days in I was transformed. Life slowed. Strangers became friends. In New Zealand I hiked glaciers, camped on beaches, learned the Southern Sky. In Australia I slept in the Outback, sailed the Whitsundays, earned my scuba license in the Great Barrier Reef. In Thailand I trekked through motorless villages, meditated with monks, learned valuable lessons in elephant welfare. In Nepal I white-water-rafted and camped where villagers had never seen a Westerner or white person. I trekked days at a time to tea houses and summited peaks.

Then I was confronted with a situation that took me to the edges of my common sense. In Brazil I saw a woman begging. She was sitting outside a pharmacy, cradling an infant. I didn't want to hand her cash, so I went inside and bought baby formula that she'd asked for. I felt as if I'd done something meaningful, but later that night someone told me that powdered baby formula was what they used to cut heroin. Dealers knew people wouldn't always give money, so they made use of other tactics. I was stunned. Then, I met a seven-year-old boy who was addicted to heroin. He staggered down the street, begging, and I offered him food. He didn't want that; he wanted money. His little body was too wired to eat, but I sat with him day after day at the same restaurant. Finally he accepted a meal at my dinner table, and then collapsed in my lap and slept. It was heartbreaking but also illuminating.

We want to help, but sometimes in our rush to be kind we bypass being wise.

I had good intentions. But good intentions built on false assumptions can do more harm than good. I had acted without the full story, without cultural context, without asking deeper questions. I let my heart lead. It can be dangerous when our empathy goes unchecked by discernment. Critical thinking isn't the opposite of compassion; it's the companion to it. It's the discipline of asking, "What else might be true? What don't I know yet?" It's a pause before reaction, a commitment to truth, not just to feeling good. We live in a world that urges reflexive responses, but truth is almost always layered. And when we don't seek the whole picture, we risk becoming part of the problem we set out to solve.

So the question I'll lead with is this: Where in your life are you acting on half the story? Empathy is powerful. But empathy guided by insight is how we change the world one act of kindness at a time.

SEEING THROUGH LENSES

I was eating in a restaurant in Vietnam when a woman with severe physical disabilities rolled in on a wooden board fitted with wheels. She had no use of one arm and both legs, but she had a stunningly beautiful voice. As she sang, the entire restaurant fell silent. Her voice was a gift. When she finished, she extended her hand, and I froze. I had a hard-and-fast rule with myself: I didn't give money. So I looked away. Then I realized that she hadn't begged. She had *offered something to earn money*. She had given the gift of her voice, and I had immediately returned to my pattern of thinking and beliefs. My skepticism had become my shield, and I'd used it to block a moment of connection and grace.

Another day, I was in the Mekong Delta, having lunch with a group of Germans. I didn't speak their language and felt invisible, irritated, and alone. I noticed a Vietnamese man standing in the doorway, staring and smiling at me. I tried to ignore him, but he didn't move; he just stood there, staring. It was uncomfortable, and I grew increasingly irritated. The lunch seemed to drag on forever. When we got up to leave, he stepped forward and grabbed my hand. Startled, I pulled back. "Thank you," he said, eyes glassy. My guide explained that the man's uncle had been saved by American soldiers during the war. When he sees an American, he waits, sometimes for hours, just to say thank you.

Thinking about that moment brings me to tears every time. I almost missed that because I didn't separate my discomfort from the reality in front of me. I didn't pause to question whether what I was feeling was true or just *familiar*. If the lunch had been enjoyable, I might've interpreted the man's presence as warm. But my irritation colored the entire frame. And that's when I understood, awareness isn't just intellectual. It's emotional. It's spiritual. It's being able to ask, *in real time*, "Am I seeing clearly? Or am I reacting from an old, unexamined, or disturbing story?" Learning to separate feelings and reactions from present truth is an awakening. I couldn't change those moments, but I could change what I brought to the next one: presence, humility, and a clearer lens.

LEARNING AS YOU GO

What I had lost and eventually found again was the balance. As I thought through my inner rule of not giving money to beggars—because a lot of them are forced to beg from an oppressor—I realized that's not critical thinking. That's pattern reactivity. Critical thinking requires something deeper. It means noticing your emotional triggers *and* questioning your cognitive shortcuts. Cognitive science tells us that the brain loves shortcuts. It makes decisions fast, based on limited data, to keep us safe. This is useful in emergencies but dangerous in human relationships.

While there is no official standard list of the skills that make up critical thinking, to me, at its core, it includes three components:

1. Clarity over certainty—the willingness to say, "I don't know yet," instead of jumping to conclusions.

2. Perspective taking—the ability to hold multiple viewpoints, especially ones that challenge your own.

3. Emotional regulation—the skill of noticing your feelings without being ruled by them.

That last one is rarely taught, but it's *essential*. Emotional reactivity is the enemy of clear thinking. When we feel anxious, defensive, or overwhelmed, the brain narrows its options. We lose focus. We stop asking questions and miss the real story.

So how do you know when to be cautious and when to be generous? You pause. You check your story. You ask, "Is this fear or fact? What else could be true here? Am I seeing this person, or projecting onto them?" You won't always get it right, but you'll *see* more clearly.

The moments we regret the most aren't when we were too cautious or too generous; they're when we weren't fully *present*, when we didn't stop long enough to *ascertain* and let our biases override our humanity.

Let Values Guide Your Truth

While I was growing up, my family moved a lot, which made me the perpetual new girl. I wanted what any thirteen-year-old wants—to belong. So at a new school when the popular girls offered me a fast track into their circle with drugs, I had a decision to make: to fit in or not. I said no. I said no because I knew it was wrong; I didn't want anything to do with that. I had my integrity.

Your integrity is your compass. Values are the internal GPS that keep you oriented when life throws detours. Without them every decision is a coin toss. But here's the key: You can't use your values as a compass unless you've taken the time to name them. You can't navigate your life wisely if you don't know what you're navigating *toward*. Values are not rules. They are deeply *felt* truths that make you feel most aligned, most whole, most *you*. What's important is not *which* values you choose but that you know them deeply and live them, consistently, because your values are not just who you are; they are the framework for *how you make decisions.*

I said no to those girls. That instinct of wanting to keep my integrity was a seed of critical thinking. Critical thinking isn't cold analysis. It's knowing what questions to ask and *who you want to be while asking them.*

- Does this choice align with what I believe in?
- Am I being swayed by fear or moved by truth?
- Am I operating with instinct and intuition?

If you want to be someone who acts with integrity, know your values. Live them when it's easy. Practice them when it's not. And when the stakes are high, it's your values that become the guide.

Producing Perspective

When I returned to the US, I built a career producing television, documentaries, and live events across all seven continents. Producing isn't just planning and organizing—it's wearing many hats through the entire production. It's the art of holding a thousand variables in your head while keeping the story on point. In other words, producing is *critical thinking in motion.*

Every shoot demands presence. Every interview requires discernment. Every unforeseen challenge—equipment lost at border crossings, a hijacked helicopter, a political uprising—becomes a moment to ask, "What matters most? How do we adapt and move forward?"

A good producer doesn't just organize. A good producer *frames.* They decide what goes in the shot and what doesn't. They make meaning from chaos. And isn't that what life demands of us, to observe and ask if our lens it too narrow?

In Europe I visited the Anne Frank House in Amsterdam many times. One year after the tour there was an interactive exhibit. A video would play, and a question appeared. You had to choose a response. The catch was that each answer had consequences. What seemed black and white wasn't. I realized that there is no right answer without context. No truth without perspective.

Critical thinking is about being *conscious*—focused awareness, advocacy, and action instead of blind activism.

That's the work I'm devoting myself to—to build a world where people think like producers, with a wide lens, brilliant edits, and authentic truth. That's why I created Erawa—*aware* spelled backward. I'm building projects that teach awareness, global perspective, and decision-making under pressure.

Living my truth wasn't a lightning strike. It was a thousand small decisions. Saying no to conformity. Saying yes to adventure. Leaving jobs. Trusting instinct. Reframing mistakes. I've gotten lost on mountains literally and metaphorically, but each time, I've found a deeper part of myself by asking better questions and listening to the answers that don't always come from my head. Critical thinking isn't just a skill. It's a way of being.

If you're on a quest to discover your own truth, you don't need to know the whole map. You just need to determine the next honest step. And dig deep for the courage to take it.

About Catherine

Catherine Cooper is a truth seeker, a global traveler, and an advocate for critical thinking as a path to clarity, compassion, and conscious decision-making.

Her journey began with a backpack and a multi-country plane ticket with stops in various countries and continents, following the sun around the world. Traveling on a budget with her home upon her back had its challenges. What she found wasn't just a way out of adversities—it was a way through. Many experiences taught her that critical thinking doesn't start with certainty. It starts in chaos. It starts out of the comfort zone, in the willingness to ask better questions when nothing feels clear.

Catherine left behind a successful television career—taking a leap into the unknown—to backpack solo to many parts of the world. She yearned to have experiences with people, not just film them. Her travels took her from the glaciers of New Zealand to the favelas of Brazil, from the Australian Outback to the red clay of Laos, from the DMZ in Vietnam to the challenges of trekking in the Himalayas, from the silence of remote temples to the noise of her own internal reckoning. Along the way she discovered that empathy without insight can mislead, and that good intentions must be guided by deeper understanding.

Her experiences, both behind the cameras and on the road, revealed a powerful truth: Critical thinking isn't cold analysis. It's the intersection of intellect and instinct, emotion and evidence, awareness and action. It's how we separate signal from noise, story from stereotype, fear from fact.

Catherine has produced television programming and live events across all seven continents. Through her company Erawa (*aware* spelled backward), she now creates content and experiences that teach emotional intelligence, decision-making under pressure, and the realization that rationale is not the same in every culture and every country. She advocates for critical thinking, among other passions, including clean water and wildlife conservation around the world. Critical thinking brings about the strongest decisions on creating awareness and action in order to advocate for any passionate causes.

Catherine helps audiences understand that truth isn't a destination—it's a practice. It's not found in quick conclusions but in the courage to pause, to get curious, and to live in alignment with one's values, even when the path is uncertain. The most important thing a person ever learns isn't what to think—it's how.

Connect with Catherine:

- erawa.net
- cooper@erawa.net

CHAPTER 10

SIGNAL BY SIGNAL

My Path to Freedom, Meaning, and Value

By Tran Tien Cong

The dread always settled in around day ten. It was a slow, sinking weight in my chest that felt like wet cement hardening with every passing hour.

My stomach would tighten up as the clock ticked closer to the day I'd get back on the ship and head offshore. One day I'd be out with friends, partying and enjoying our time on land. The next, I'd head back to what I called the jungle—two weeks on an isolated oil rig, followed by two weeks off.

On the surface everything looked good. I had a high-paying job. I owned a home. By society's standards I was successful. But success started to feel more like a costume I wore than a truth I lived.

This wasn't the life I imagined for myself. When I was eighteen, I dreamed of being a teacher. I loved teaching and helping others, but at the time, I didn't have the opportunity or the support. My father, who was practical and well-meaning, told me to study something predictable. So I studied mechanical engineering, got the job, and followed the script.

On paper it was perfect, but paper can't measure purpose. I could feel that something was missing. My top values are freedom, meaning, and impact, and I wasn't living any of those.

For years I convinced myself that the money made it worth it. In my country having a stable job, a wife, kids, and a home is the benchmark for success. But deep down I was going through the motions, watching my energy drain out day by day. And I wasn't alone. I saw friends working themselves to the bone for fifteen years, too afraid to walk away from the security even if it was killing their spirit. That was the part that scared me the most: how *normal* it had become to live this way.

Then, one night in 2011, as the next offshore shift loomed like a dark cloud, I couldn't ignore my truth anymore.

I knew that if I kept living this way, nothing would change. And that realization hit me like a lightning bolt. The heaviness in my mind was crushing to the point that I felt in my soul that I had just two choices: change or die.

WHAT YOUR TRUTH REQUIRES

At first it's just a whisper. A growing sense of discomfort. A quiet voice that says, "This isn't it. There's more."

Most people ignore it. They convince themselves that they should be happy with what they have, but that inner knowing never goes away. It only gets louder until it becomes impossible to ignore.

That's where I was in 2011 when I made the riskiest decision of my life. I invested $6,000 in a personal development program. That was a big investment for me, equal to six months of salary. I had no idea what it would lead to. I couldn't explain the outcome to anyone else, not even to myself. I just knew *something* had to change.

My first investment was in Jack Canfield's Personal Success coaching program, then Tony Robbins Result Coaching. At the time, there was no coaching industry at all in Vietnam, but I felt deeply pulled to being a motivational speaker. My coach encouraged me to attend coaching school in Canada. I started coaching my friends and saw them change. What I discovered was this: If your truth leads you to something that lights you up, *follow it*, even if the impact seems small at first.

Coaching one-on-one was fulfilling, but I knew the impact could be bigger; I could change thousands of lives and create a movement here. I decided to launch the Vietnam Coaching Institute, the *first* of its kind in my country.

I had no business background, no safety net, and no plan except for the one my soul gave me. And that's often how truth works. It doesn't give you a map; it gives you a *direction*.

A year into running the school, I was $25,000 in debt. I had to return to corporate work to pay it off and felt as if I had failed. I wondered if I should give up on my dream. I worked in oil and gas by day and worked on my dream by night. Then came a moment I'll never forget. A friend pulled me aside and said, "The CEO heard you're doing something else on the side. Be careful. You could get fired."

Something in me *snapped*.

I had always believed that success meant a stable job and a steady paycheck, but in that moment, I saw the truth: No job is truly secure. If I wanted real freedom—emotional, financial, spiritual—I'd have to create it myself.

That day, I made a commitment to myself. I would stop outsourcing my safety and build my own foundation. I would go *all in*.

I've learned that our truth doesn't work halfway. If you're half in, you'll get half the results. If you're waiting for the "right time," you'll wait forever. Your truth requires your full attention, your full heart, your full courage.

And it *will* speak to you. A restlessness. A gut feeling. A moment of sudden clarity. These aren't coincidences. They are *signals* that your truth is trying to reach you.

Signal 1: A Restlessness You Can't Explain

One of the clearest signs that your truth is speaking is this: You're willing to *complicate* your life in pursuit of something that feels more authentic.

My friends were content. They had good salaries and decent lifestyles, and they didn't question it. I thought maybe the problem was *me*. Why couldn't I just be satisfied like they were? Why did I have this sense that something was missing? Why was I obsessed with complicating a life that on paper was already "good"?

That's a signal. If you're willing to risk the predictable path for something uncertain but meaningful, and disrupt stability in service to a calling you can't explain—that's your truth trying to get your attention.

The turning point came when I realized that my life didn't lack money; it lacked meaning. And I was willing to pay the price to find it.

It's as Jack Canfield teaches in *The Success Principles*, "Joy is the signal."

That doesn't mean the absence of stress. It means that even in the middle of risk, there's a deep sense of joy. You are pursuing something worth the tension it takes to get there. Truth isn't always convenient, but it's *undeniable*.

If you find yourself wondering why you can't just be satisfied, listen closely. Your life is trying to tell you something.

Signal 2: You're Scared

Fear is often misunderstood. Most people think fear means to stop, that they're doing something wrong. They think fear means they aren't ready. But I've learned the opposite is true. Fear often shows up not because you're on the wrong path but because you are finally getting close on the *right* one.

When I first started following my dream in 2011, I looked up to Tony Robbins. His energy and message inspired me. I wanted to be a speaker too, but the thought of getting up in front of a crowd made my hands shake with nervousness. A few years passed, and my company began to feel more like an event company than a business. I relied heavily on international experts to lead the programs, but in 2016 I realized that if I wanted VCI to grow, I had to become the expert myself. That decision was terrifying, so that's where I went.

I joined Toastmasters and BNI. Every week I had to give a speech, and for two years I was terrified, but I kept showing up. I *wanted* to be heard. I wanted to add value. And reach more people.

Fear wasn't a stop sign. It was a signal that I was stepping into something bigger.

I stepped up, trained, spoke, and became the face of the company. VCI became the number one coaching school in Vietnam. Fear doesn't mean you're not capable; it just means you haven't built the skills—*yet*.

The more I practiced, the more my confidence grew. Many people say you have to kill the fear, but I think fear is always there when we're growing into something bigger than we've experienced before. I didn't eliminate the fear; I learned how to *play* with it and use it as motivation. Fear is just the pull between who you are now and who you're becoming. It's the *cost* of living your truth but also the compass.

In fact, fear and excitement often live side by side. If a dream doesn't scare you, it's probably not big enough. Fear is not the enemy. It's the invitation.

Signal 3: You Feel Proud

There's a quiet, unmistakable feeling that shows up when you're living your truth. It's *pride*—not ego or arrogance, but a deep, grounded knowing that you're showing up and that even in the hard moments—*especially* in the hard moments—you're still walking toward the life you're meant for.

I've had seasons where I worked harder than I ever did in corporate. Long nights. Heavy responsibility. But somehow it all felt *lighter*. There was joy and alignment. When you're living your truth, there's a fire inside you that doesn't burn you out; it *fuels* you. You're pulled forward by something deeper than duty, and in those moments, even when no one else sees your effort, you feel proud. That feeling is a signal.

When your truth is speaking, it doesn't just feel exciting or scary; it also feels *honorable*. Pride is one of the greatest rewards of living your truth because it goes hand in hand with self-love. No trophy, title, or paycheck can match the feeling of knowing you've had the courage to take a stand for your dream.

If I asked you right now, "What do you do?" what would you feel most proud to say? Your answer is your truth.

Signal 4: It Doesn't Make Logical Sense

When your truth starts to lead the way, it will often take you in a direction that defies logic. It won't always come with a clear plan or add up on paper, but somehow you *know*. That was me in 2011, standing on the edge of a decision that made no sense at all. Back then coaching was virtually unknown in Vietnam. I didn't fully understand what it was. I didn't know how it would help me, and I certainly didn't have the money to spare.

But I had something else—*intuition*, a quiet certainty that this was part of my future. So I took the leap, not because it made sense but because it *didn't*. That single, illogical decision changed my life. I didn't know then that I would go on to build Vietnam's first coaching institute and go from coaching twenty people to thousands. I didn't know that I'd coauthor a book with Jack Canfield, the same man whose work inspired my journey.

But I had *vision*.

In one coaching exercise, I wrote down that I would become a best-selling author. I didn't know *how*, but I believed it was a matter of *when*, not *if*. When your deepest desires make no sense, pay close attention. That's often the clearest signal of all. Logic keeps you where you are. *Intuition* pulls you toward where you're meant to go.

Signal 5: When Conviction Is Louder Than Circumstance

Sometimes your truth doesn't feel light or exciting. Sometimes it feels like a fight. That's how I felt in 2020.

My business was built entirely on live, in-person events. When COVID hit, it all came to a halt. A lot of business owners paused. Others waited for things to "go back to normal." But something inside me said, "Move. Now!"

I let go of the office and went digital. People told me it wouldn't work, that coaching and training couldn't be done effectively online, and that no one would pay for a virtual experience. But

I knew the world was shifting. I didn't have proof, but I had *conviction*.

We hosted our first online event, and it worked. While others were still hoping things would go back, I built forward. I 4x-ed my business! Before the pandemic, I trained eight to ten students per workshop. After moving online, I consistently trained thirty-five to forty students per event, at $2,000 each! My business became more profitable, more scalable, and more aligned than ever, and none of it would have happened without that *stubborn resolve*.

When logic said to wait, I trusted the signal that said, "Keep going."

The world will test your truth. It will throw uncertainty, loss, fear, and doubt, but if your truth is real, it won't let you quit. Trust that what you're feeling isn't just a hunch; it's a *signal*.

TRUST THE SIGNALS. TRUST YOURSELF.

One of the most life-changing books I've ever read is *Awaken the Giant Within* by Tony Robbins. There's a quote in that book that still lives in me: "It's in your moments of decision that your destiny is shaped."

That's exactly what this journey has been for me—a series of decisions. Some small. Some terrifying, but each one led me closer to the life I was meant to live.

If I hadn't had the courage to change my own life, I would've never changed anyone else's. If I had ignored those truth signals— the fear, the vision, the pride, the conviction—I would have stayed stuck in a version of success that looked good but felt empty.

Over the past thirteen years, I've invested hundreds of thousands of dollars into personal growth and worked with world-class mentors, not because I wanted a collection of certifications but because I believe in growing every day. I believe in the wisdom of mentors who can help me become a better, wiser, and more impactful human.

I don't just teach personal development. I *live* it. And if I could give you just one piece of advice, it's this: Find a coach. This will be one of the most important decisions you'll ever make in your life. Surround yourself with people who see more in you than you can see in yourself. The truth is already in you, and the signals are already speaking.

That quiet pull toward purpose. That flicker of pride when you envision it all coming to fruition. The fear that shows up right before your biggest breakthrough. The resolve that rises when everything seems to be falling apart.

Those are your truth signals. And when you learn to trust them, you learn to trust *yourself.*

You don't have to know the whole map. Just trust the next signal. That's how you begin to live your truth.

That's when life truly begins. And that's when the giant within you finally wakes up.

About Cong

Founder, Vietnam Coaching Institute (VCI) Certified Executive Coach | Peak Performance Coach | ICF-Certified Coach Trainer | Master Coach

Tran Tien Cong is the founder of the Vietnam Coaching Institute (VCI)—the first organization in Vietnam to provide professional coaching certification programs aligned with the standards of the International Coaching Federation (ICF). Since 2012 he has been recognized as a pioneer who laid the foundation for the coaching profession in Vietnam, with a vision to establish coaching as both a sustainable career path and a conscious way of living. Cong is a master coach with more than thirty-five hundred hours of coaching experience, working with leaders, entrepreneurs, and aspiring coaches across diverse industries.

Over the past thirteen years he has trained and mentored more than two thousand leaders and professional coaches, supporting them in mastering core coaching skills, developing a strong professional mindset, and building successful coaching businesses. He is widely regarded as the top-of-mind mentor for anyone in Vietnam looking to build a serious and sustainable coaching career—the one people seek out when they are ready to go professional. He is also affectionately known as Coach's Mentor for his role in shaping multiple generations of Vietnamese coaches.

He is the first Vietnamese author to write three in-depth books on coaching:

- *The Journey to Becoming a Professional Coach*
- *Freelance Coach*
- *Launch Your Solopreneur Career with Coaching Skills*

These works are praised for their clarity, practicality, and ability to shape the mindset and method of new coaches in Vietnam.

In addition, Cong is the creator of two highly effective and easy-to-apply frameworks:

- Inspirational Coaching Matrix—a twelve-step model that helps coaches confidently deliver transformational results for clients.

- Closing Matrix—an eight-step sales system that turns leads into paying clients, often boosting closing rates and revenue by 30 to 100 percent.

He holds certifications from globally respected organizations such as Marshall Goldsmith Stakeholder Centered Coaching, John Mattone Intelligent Leadership Coaching, and Tony Robbins Coach Training. He has delivered coaching and leadership programs for leading corporations, including AEON, P&G, Heineken, PepsiCo, Techcombank, and Prudential.

Beyond his professional life, Cong enjoys reading, learning from global thought leaders, and watching Premier League football. He enjoys a peaceful, grounded life with his wife, Willow, their two daughters, Moon and May, and their little dog, Chu Chu.

Learn more about Cong:

Website: https://vcicoach.com
Facebook: https://www.facebook.com/tran.t.cong.9
LinkedIn: https://www.linkedin.com/in/trantiencongcoaching/

CHAPTER 11

IS YOUR GPS TURNED ON?

By Rosemary Blaum

Every day thousands of people miss their destiny. They feel a nudge, an inner voice that whispers a command. "Don't take that trip," it might say. "Go to this city." "Quit this job." It arrives uninvited, compelling and illogical all at once. And often it's dismissed as a fluke, just another stray thought that doesn't make any sense. What if that whisper *isn't* just a random thought? What if it's divine intelligence disguised as instinct? What if it's God's probing sensor? A sacred breadcrumb pointing you toward your truth, your purpose, your fate?

For me, that voice hit me out of the blue when everything in my life was going great. I was running a successful design firm, I sat on the mayor's council, attended all the key events, and enjoyed all the trimmings of a prosperous life. On the outside I had what most people wanted, but on the inside I knew there was something missing, a family. I had always imagined that I would have a house full of children. *Why wasn't this happening?* I resolved that it just wasn't meant to be.

Then, out of nowhere, something stirred deep within my soul, and I knew I was supposed to move and leave my life in Texas. The sense of urgency was strong. "Move to North Carolina," my inner voice called. I didn't understand it, but I knew I had to listen. My friends thought I was having a midlife crisis. No one understood how I could walk away from clients like General Dynamics, the Dallas Cowboys, AT&T, and the like. Some things can't be explained with logic, but that doesn't mean it's not the right decision. Have you ever just *known* something, but you couldn't say why? That's the way it was for me. So when the voice said, "Go," I did.

As soon as I pulled up to the tiny, four-hundred-square-foot cabin tucked deep in the mountains, a neighbor I hardly knew tapped on my car window. "We have a baby for you," she said to my astonishment. "We've been waiting for you!" *Could this be true, or is it a hoax?* In just three weeks the baby would be born, and I'd become a mother! Suddenly, it all made sense. *This* was why I was pulled here. My son was here waiting for me. My intuition knew what my rational mind couldn't possibly have known.

When he was born, it was the most joyful moment of my life. But as the nurses lifted him up, my heart sank. He was beautiful, but he was blue.

Your Truth Comes in Bits and Pieces

For years I lived as a version of myself that wasn't quite me. As a child, I was expressive, imaginative, and full of life, yet often told, "You're too much—tone it down." The message was clear: Well-behaved girls are quiet, agreeable, and easy to manage. I learned that if I wanted to be loved, I needed to shrink. So I did. I dimmed my light, quieted my voice, and disappeared into who I thought I *should* be. That decision followed me into adulthood.

The real turning point came when my son was born. When a child is deprived of oxygen at birth, they enter the world blue. The impact is lifelong, reshaping their path and the lives of those who love them. A simple task becomes one full of hurdles to jump through. Suddenly, my goals shifted from personal achievements to understanding my child's mind and heart and the quiet wisdom of his soul. I set about studying the brain's remarkable ability to change, reorganize, and even reroute pathways to compensate for damage and form new habits that help us adapt and function in life. This was powerful! I soon realized that my son was a gift, a catalyst to help me explore the diverse differences in people and understand why they do what they do. Without me realizing it, my career was taking me on a whole new road. I never would have thought that I'd spend the next fifteen years studying the brain and developing techniques that take people from where they are to where they want to be.

My son showed me that truth can be quiet, steady, and deeply powerful, and he awakened in me a fascination with the brain that shaped not only how I parent but how I motivate, coach, and teach leadership strategies. We all have our own unique pathway to finding our authentic self. It's not always loud. It doesn't have to look like anyone else's. It just has to be *real*. It's often the detours, disruptions, and unplanned paths that bring us back to the parts of ourselves we were meant to remember. Truth comes in pieces. And when we slow down enough to listen, *really* listen, we start to find those missing pieces one moment, one choice, *one* challenge at a time.

There *are* steps you can take to uncover your truth more deliberately. I've outlined each of the seven steps in my book, *Is Your GPS Turned On?* But here's where it begins: With curiosity, with permission, and with the courage to ask, "What if I stopped performing and started becoming?"

DEFINE THE DESTINATION, THEN WORK BACKWARD

At one point in my life I was the corporate construction design manager for Marriott Vacation Club. The pace was fast, the stakes were high, and my days were full of decisions that affected millions of dollars in revenue. Something I learned in that high-pressure world of project management applies to life outside the boardroom, especially when it comes to finding your truth: You have to start with the end in mind. Once you know what makes you tick and lights you up, you can build a "critical path" by starting from the end and working backward.

The critical path is the series of steps and potential obstacles that determine whether you'll get to the outcome on time. At Marriott

I had to know what holidays would delay a project, which contractors might fall behind, and what to do if permits didn't come through in time for deadlines. I had to see it *before* it happened and have backup plans in place. Life works the same way.

If your "project" is selling a house before the end of the year, you must account for holidays, school breaks, weather, and repairs. If your goal is stepping into your truth by next spring, you must look ahead: What might derail you? Who or what might pull you back into old patterns? What actions can be put in place now to stay on track? Declare what matters. Declare what you want. And then, with control and flexibility, work backward—while walking forward—with strong intention, determination, and a faithful heart.

FEEL THE FEAR—AND DO IT ANYWAY

Truth doesn't always arrive in calm reflection. Sometimes it roars through chaos when the stakes are high, fear is loud, and trust in your decision is the only way forward. Years ago I was managing a high-stakes Fortune 500 project in Aruba. I didn't realize the entire island would shut down for ten days over Easter. No cargo. No backups. No one coming to save me. For a moment I froze. If I didn't make this work, I'd be fired. The thought of being an unemployed single mom was not something I was willing to accept. Then a quiet voice rose up inside me: "You can do this. Find a way." I took a breath and started moving. I made calls and pieced together a plan, communicating in a language I barely spoke. I rallied my team and negotiated with decision-makers, and miraculously the cargo was released. Hours later the final pieces were installed just in time for the grand opening.

That moment taught me that success isn't about flawless plans. It's about grit, resourcefulness, and remembering that pressure doesn't break you; it *reveals* you. Fear will always be there, but it doesn't have to be the loudest voice. Send it to the back, and trust yourself to find a way through.

When you're facing your own version of a locked cargo door, ask yourself, "What happens if I don't try? Can I accept that? And what might happen if I do?"

Take a breath and step forward. Listen to your intuition. The path to your truth isn't paved in ease. Sometimes it's forged on a hot island tarmac with your back against the wall and your future in your own two hands.

Sometimes No Is an Invitation to Step Deeper into Your Truth

The word *no* doesn't always mean stop. Sometimes the harshest rejections are sacred invitations to rise. I still remember what my professor, Mrs. Schwartz, said the day I turned in my first design project in college. It wasn't my best work, but instead of owning that, I made excuses, blaming the deadline, the workload, anything but myself. Mrs. Schwartz looked at the project and said, "This degree path is not for you. You don't have what it takes. Go find something else." Her words hit like a slap. I felt devastated and defeated. But after a couple of days, something unexpected happened. A quiet conviction started to rise. I wanted this path, and therefore I just needed to find a way. "I can do better than this," I told myself. *"And I will."*

That moment became a turning point. I stopped treating my path like a maybe. I got disciplined and focused and worked harder than I ever had before. Then came the final semester and with it my final project. I poured myself into it for days. No shortcuts. No excuses. When Mrs. Schwartz looked at the finished work, she studied it in silence and then said, "I'm glad you didn't take my advice." I smiled back and said, "Your *no* pushed me to rise to the level I knew I was capable of. Without that opportunity I might have remained a C student. But instead, I found my excellence."

That day taught me something powerful: Sometimes the people who doubt us are unknowingly guiding us back to our truth. Not every closed door is a curse. Not every rejection is meant to stop you. Some are meant to *wake you up*.

Too many people drift through life accepting average as good enough. But sometimes it takes a sharp no to show you what you're really made of. We all hold the key that unlocks the door to our future.

The question is, Will you use it? Will you take the no, the rejection, the doubt and use it to retreat, or will you use it to rise and face tomorrow with determination and grit? Sometimes the most powerful version of your true, authentic self is waiting for you on the other side of someone else's disbelief.

SOMETIMES THE SETBACK IS THE SETUP

When the road you thought was yours begins to crumble, it may not be failure. It may be divine redirection into your next journey. I had just stepped into what I believed would be a fulfilling new chapter. I accepted a role with a national company whose mission deeply resonated with me. I was energized and imagined it would be a long, meaningful season in my career. But as time went on, something felt off. The harder I worked, the more resistance I encountered. The time and the energy I poured in wasn't bearing fruit. I started to wonder why nothing was working. Had I misread the signs? Was this not the right path? And underneath those questions a quieter voice whispered: "What about your book?" "What about your coaching?" "How much longer will you keep putting your purpose on hold?" Still, I stayed. I rationalized. I hoped it would turn around—until one day, when the call came: My role was ending. Just like that, the door closed. At first, I felt as if I had failed. I questioned everything. But in the quiet that followed, I brought my disappointment and my weary heart to God, and in that sacred stillness I was reminded of a promise I had made to myself: to finish what I had started. To write the book that had been living inside me. To help others break free from self-doubt and self-sabotage and finally step into the life they were meant to live. And with that remembrance came peace. The truth was, I hadn't failed. I'd been redirected.

That closed door didn't take me off course. It *was* the course correction, the very thing that forced me to stop detouring around my deeper calling. Purpose has a way of pursuing you. And if you ignore it long enough, life will find a way to bring you back to it.

Stepping into your purpose won't always feel like the safe choice, but it will always lead you to your most honest, most authentic self. So if you're facing a setback, pause before labeling it a failure. It might just be the setup you need for your next evolution. The door you're meant to walk through isn't always the one you picked. But it will always lead you back to your true self.

YOUR TRUTH WAS NEVER LOST—ONLY WAITING

It's never too late for a new beginning. Throughout life people will hand you keys disguised as advice. "Try this path." "Stick to what you're good at." "Don't make a change now." But if the door doesn't feel right, it probably isn't yours.

I spent years trying to unlock the life others envisioned for me until I finally reached for the key that had been in my own pocket all along. The moment I stopped performing and started listening to God, to my soul, to the quiet knowing inside me, I didn't just survive; I came alive. And I realized something important: You don't have to become someone new. You simply have to return to who you've always been.

I've taken detours. I've said yes when I should've said no. I've ignored my instincts and lost myself in the noise. But I've also learned to pause. To listen. To recalibrate. And most importantly, to trust my own voice.

Then came one of my greatest teachers: my son. I used to ask God in frustration, "What were You thinking?" Now I know exactly what He was thinking. He is the child I needed to grow in every way I didn't know I lacked. He taught me patience, compassion, and how to love someone as they are, not as I hoped they'd be. In helping him find his way, I found more of mine.

That's the work I do now. To help people come home to themselves. To live their lives full out. With purpose. With heart. With truth. Not by becoming someone new but by returning to who they've always been, beneath all the noise. Your truth is already here, quiet, steady, patient. All it's waiting for is *you*.

About Rosemary

When people meet Rosemary Blaum, one thing becomes immediately clear: She is passionate about helping others rise above life's challenges and reconnect with their full potential. With over thirty years of experience in leadership, communication, and personal development, she empowers individuals to build confidence, develop strong leadership skills, and go after lives that truly light them up!

A certified Success Principles trainer with Jack Canfield, Rosemary has studied under his guidance and brings that same life-changing wisdom into her own coaching. When the opportunity came up to coauthor *Living Truth* with Jack, she jumped at the chance.

Her coaching is rooted in the belief that it's not the setbacks we face that shape us but how we respond that makes all the difference. With a background in neuroscience, brain health, and communication and interpersonal skills, Rosemary helps people move beyond the daily grind and step into a more fulfilling and purposeful life.

She holds a master's degree in organizational leadership and development, as well as numerous certifications in life coaching, communications, conflict resolution, and project management. Before stepping into coaching full time, Rosemary built a successful career in interior design, earning national recognition and two awards for innovative designs. Today, that same creative spark now fuels work helping others "design" lives from the inside out—lives that reflect who they truly are.

Often called the Inside Out Coach, Rosemary is known for her mix of compassion, strategy, and straight talk to help people break through limiting beliefs, reset their mindsets, and create lasting transformation. Whether leading a workshop, coaching one-on-one, or facilitating a corporate training, she delivers practical tools and powerful insights to help others live and lead authentically—and thrive like never before.

Through her coaching and writing, Rosemary reminds us it's never too late to realign your life with your deepest values and ignite your dreams. Her upcoming book, *Is Your GPS Turned On?*, explores the power of intuition as an internal guide to living a more meaningful, purpose-filled life.

When she's not coaching or speaking, you'll find Rosemary cruising through a city on a Segway, riding a mountain train, kayaking through mangroves, or attending a lively music concert. Her motto? *Life is an adventure—enjoy every minute you can!*

To connect with Rosemary or learn more about what she's up to, reach out to her—she'd love to hear from you!

Facebook: Rosemary Olivia Blaum
Email: rose@rosemaryblaum.com
Instagram: @rosemary.blaum
Website: https://rosemaryblaum.com

CHAPTER 12

SAY MY NAME

Honoring Your Identity, Your Dreams, and Your Truth

By Tameika L. Chambers-Pope

T hey called me Tammy. And every time they did, something in me recoiled—not because Tammy is a bad name but because it wasn't mine.

It wasn't the name my mother gave me. It wasn't the name that matched the rhythm of my spirit. It was a name I started using when the world told me that "Tameika" would never get me in the door.

I was young, qualified, and hungry! I'd done everything right. I studied hard, graduated, and built a résumé I was proud of. But the phone never rang. At first, I thought maybe I wasn't good enough, but then a recruiter friend said what I hadn't dared to consider: "They're not calling you back because your name is Tameika. Unless they're *looking* for a Black girl, they're not going to hire one." That sentence cut through me like a knife.

She told me to change my name to Tammy on my résumé and resend it. Just like that, my phone started ringing off the hook. It floored me, but more than that, it called my truth into question. Because Tammy wasn't just a name; it was a mask, and every time I wore it, I felt smaller. More accepted, perhaps, but less *seen*. When I finally got the job and they called me Tammy in the office, it hit differently. At first, I didn't correct them, but the more they said it, the more it hurt. One day I finally said, "My name is Tameika." I remember the way the syllables felt in my mouth, solid and unapologetic. That was the moment I reclaimed something sacred.

That experience changed everything. It lit the spark that led me to become a recruiter not just because I understood the system but because I wanted to *change* it. I didn't want another qualified, worthy soul to be passed over because their name made someone uncomfortable. What I didn't know then was that this wasn't just about recruiting. The universe was laying bricks beneath bigger purpose—to use my voice so others could find theirs. Even naming my children became a form of reclamation. Both my daughters have bold, unisex names, names that don't immediately reveal race or gender. I didn't want the paper to define them before their presence could.

That single act of reclaiming my name became a spiritual awakening. It taught me that our names carry more than phonetics. They carry identity. History. Dignity. Truth. And truth? It has a way of showing up in life's most jarring moments. Sometimes quietly. Sometimes like an earthquake. But always with a message: *This is who you are.* Living your truth starts with a decision to be who you are even when it costs you. Even when it's uncomfortable. Even when it means correcting the world one syllable at a time.

Our truth doesn't always arrive gently. It often breaks through in the moments that shake us most. Good or bad, those moments reveal the raw essence of who we are and the path we're here to walk.

ROCK THE BOAT

Sometimes you're under control and don't even know it. You're moving through life, following rituals you never questioned, traditions you don't understand, and you don't stop to ask, "Why am I doing this? Do I even want this?" That's the thing about expectations. Sometimes they dress up as culture, family, and love.

I grew up in a family where holidays were *everything*. Christmas wasn't just a celebration; it was a production. My grandparents' house was the epicenter. Everyone came, everyone cooked, and everyone played their part. And from the time I was small, I knew I wanted no part of being in the kitchen, not because it was degrading or menial but because it didn't bring me the joy it seemed to bring everyone else. While everyone else passed down recipes like heirlooms, I was passing the time until I could escape the kitchen. I didn't know why; I just *hated it*. The shopping, the chaos, standing for hours over a stove just to be too tired to enjoy the meal—none of it resonated. It wasn't just disinterest; it was *resentment*.

I got married and had kids, and still that resistance lingered. I can't count how many arguments my husband and I had about who was cooking and why I didn't want to. I remember one night I asked him to leave my grandparents' house over a fight that started with dinner but was really about *duty*. Here's what I finally realized: I was never mad at the food. I was mad at the *expectation* that said, "This is just what families do. This is what love looks like."

For me it wasn't like that, and I couldn't help but wonder if perhaps we'd confused tradition with truth. So many of the values my family held tightly, so many of the things they demonstrated as mattering, weren't born of passion—they were born of *pattern*. They did it because their parents did it. Their parents did it because *survival* demanded it. But joy? Joy wasn't always part of the recipe. And that's the part that finally snapped me out of it.

I realized that I was allowed to say no. I was allowed to redefine what holidays looked like. I was allowed to build new traditions with my own family that didn't require me to lose myself. We talk a lot about freedom, but real freedom comes when you look at something everyone around you accepts and you dare to ask, "Is this true for me?"

Truth isn't always inherited. Sometimes it has to be *forged*. So yes, I'll rock that boat. I'll let go of guilt. I'll trade the casserole for conversation, and the apron for authenticity. And I'll teach my children that just because it's expected doesn't mean it's right for them. Tradition is not a synonym for truth.

BOUNDARIES ARE NOT BETRAYALS

When I was a child, I was always on the move. My mother used to say, "All you want to do is go, go, go. You can't keep still!" I've always had a curious spirit, and I wanted to see things and go places, especially the beach. Something about water made me feel connected, free, and alive!

As I got older, that longing didn't fade. I took jobs that allowed me to travel. I prioritized experiences over stuff. I chased oceans like some people chase status. But I also grew up with a very specific kind of womanhood modeled for me. "Once you have kids," my mother would say, "you sacrifice." My mother didn't go on vacations regularly. I'm grateful for the intention behind that sacrifice, but I also knew that I didn't want that to be my story. When I had kids of my own, it came up again. My children participated in every extracurricular activity. Every week was packed with practices, recitals, or social events. And the expectation was that I should never miss a moment. My mother's sentiment was, "Moms don't miss things; moms sacrifice."

But what if I didn't believe in either/or? What if I believed in both/and? I wanted to be present for my children, but I also knew something my mother never seemed to demonstrate:

If my cup is empty, my love comes strained. And for me, travel was more than a luxury. It was how I breathed. So I made a choice. A messy one at first. I started lying. If I was flying to Miami, I'd say I was going for work. And I was, but I'd extend the trip and spend a day or two at the beach. I'd hide it because I didn't want the judgment or the guilt trip. I didn't want to feel as if I had to defend my peace. For years I operated in a kind of truth-adjacent way until one day I stopped. I stopped shrinking. Stopped apologizing. Stopped asking for permission to live a life that made sense to *me*. It wasn't easy, but I learned that boundaries aren't betrayals; they're bridges that connect who you've been to who you're becoming. Yes, my mother sacrificed, and yes, I honor that.

But I am not her. And she does not get to define my version of motherhood, womanhood, or worth.

Sometimes we have to get OK with the noise and the judgment because here's the real question: Is it more shameful to leave for a weekend, or to live a life in quiet resentment, in constant depletion, in the shadow of someone else's story? I chose my truth, and the beach, every time.

EVOLVE ANYWAY

When my marriage was ending, I did something people didn't expect. I fought for it.

I'd been with my husband for thirty years. We had built a life and raised children. When I felt us slipping apart, and had discovered why, I didn't run; I leaned in. I said, "Let's try. Let's work on this." I didn't do it because I was desperate but because *love*, to me, is worth fighting for. There was no shame in wanting to preserve what we built, especially once we learned that our problems were fixable. But when I told people, even my husband and his family, they looked at me with disbelief. "Have you lost your dignity?" they asked. "Why are you begging to save something that's done?" "Where is your pride?" And for a moment I entertained their opinions. I felt ashamed for wanting to stay and try, with new perspective on the issues. But here's what I know now: There is no shame in fighting for what you love. The shame is in quieting your truth to make other people comfortable. I knew that there was a third party in our marriage that neither of us recognized at the time. That third party was unspoken struggle. All the things we never said. The quiet assumptions, the emotional fatigue, the issues we each kept quiet, sometimes out of ignorance and sometimes out of choice.

When my husband looked at me and said, "This isn't you," something rose up inside me. It sparked a kind of defiance in me, not against him but against the stories I'd been told—that asking to try was weakness. That feeling was shameful. That grief was indulgent. I decided then and there to let go of the rules and ideas about what dignity looks like, what pride should cost, and what defines strength. And I realized something else too: Truth is about permission to shift, permission to be soft, to be brave, and to grow out of the version of you who stayed silent and into the one who finally speaks.

YOU DON'T HAVE TO BE PERFECT TO BE POWERFUL

It was 2007, and I had just landed a high-level role at a global Wall Street firm—vice president, the only Black woman in leadership at that tier. On paper I was thriving. In my bones I was carrying the weight of two worlds. I knew I was qualified and had earned a seat at the table. Yet every day, I walked into that building thinking, "You can't mess up. You're representing your race and your gender!" I was trying to speak the language and play the game perfectly because I thought perfection was the only way to keep the seat. Then, one morning, everything changed.

I was driving to work, listening to the radio. The conversation was about Dr. Martin Luther King Jr.—not his leadership but his alleged infidelities. The host was questioning whether King's legacy should still hold weight if he hadn't lived a morally flawless personal life. And then Dr. Michael Eric Dyson, a guest on the show, said something that pierced through all the noise in my mind: Does one have to be perfect to be useful?

That sentence cracked something open in me. Up until that moment my entire life had been built around chasing perfection. Growing up, if I brought home a C, my father would ask why it wasn't an A. If I said I was struggling, it was considered an excuse. What I internalized was that anything less than perfect was failing. So I overachieved my entire life. I tried to be the perfect wife, the perfect mother, the perfect professional. And it was killing me. I didn't realize how exhausted I was until that morning in the car, hearing someone say out loud what I never gave myself permission to believe: You don't have to be perfect to be useful.

That quote became my mantra. It gave me permission to fail, to rest, to admit I didn't know everything and didn't need to. People didn't need my perfection. They needed my *presence*. Now I teach my children the same thing I wish someone had told me: Do your best, yes. But don't confuse *perfection* with *power*. One will keep you trapped. The other will set you free. Usefulness leaves a legacy that flawlessness never could. I wouldn't have ventured into half the bold, beautiful things I've done in my life if I hadn't heard that quote on a drive to work.

I let go of the weight. And I picked up my truth.

I Am All Things

I used to think I had to choose between power and softness, between motherhood and ambition, between tradition and self-expression, and between being accepted and being *real*.

But I no longer believe in either/or. I believe in *all*.

I am not one thing. I am *many*. I am the woman who loves old-school R&B and classic rock. The woman who prays boldly and questions deeply. The woman who once begged for her marriage and now fiercely defends her boundaries. I've come to learn that truth is not a fixed destination. It's a living, breathing companion that shifts as we grow. The truth I lived at twenty is not the truth I walk in today. And the story I tell today may be revised tomorrow, not because it was false but because I am evolving. That's not hypocrisy. That's *honesty*.

Real truth—*living* truth—requires courage. It asks you to stand tall in rooms where you were taught to shrink and to allow yourself to be misunderstood. Here's what I know for sure: You only begin to *live* your truth when you stop asking for permission to want what you want, when you can look shame in the face and say, "Not today," when you stop performing the version of yourself that makes everyone else comfortable and start becoming the version that sets *you* free.

I am not just one thing. I am all things. And so are you.

I invite you to live boldly, to ask for what you want. Tell the hard truth, even if it fractures your familiar world. Claim your joy, even when it makes others uncomfortable.

Living truthfully isn't always easy—but it's always worth it. And every time you choose your truth, you light the way for someone else to choose theirs.

About Tameika

Tameika L. Chambers-Pope is a dynamic personal and professional development executive whose career boldly bridges the worlds of Wall Street finance, K Street government, Broadway theater, and the modern entrepreneurial journey to Silicon Valley's spirit of innovation. With over two decades of diverse experience, she brings a unique perspective to the art of transformation, resilience, and authentic leadership. Most recently, Tameika coauthored the best-selling book *Unstoppable: Stories of Grit, Determination, and Perseverance*, earning a 2025 Quill Award and further establishing her as a rising voice in empowerment literature.

As the founder of Cultivate to Great, a coaching and inspirational speaking business, Tameika helps individuals and organizations uncover their authentic path to success by first mastering self-awareness. Through powerful storytelling rooted in her personal journey—from adversity and loss to healing, self-realization, and joy—she lights a path for others to embrace resilience and live boldly. Her talks are known for sparking emotional breakthroughs and lasting mindset shifts, creating unforgettable experiences for audiences of all kinds.

Tameika's work has garnered national attention, including features in *Essence Magazine*, *Diversity Woman Magazine*, *The SheSuite*, *Women to Watch Media*, and *Beyond the Book*. In fall 2025 she will appear on *Breakthrough with Lisa Nichols*, sharing her story and insights with a broader audience. With a degree in mass media communications and journalism, along with certification as a professional life coach, she brings both credibility and relatability to her roles as speaker, author, emcee, panelist, and host.

Deeply committed to social impact, Tameika serves as a board member for the oldest domestic violence shelter in Washington, DC, advocating for women's safety, voice, and empowerment. She is passionate about helping women and emerging leaders break generational cycles, overcome fear, and create new legacies rooted in confidence and clarity. Her signature approach blends soulful inspiration with actionable strategy—empowering others not only to dream but to manifest.

A proud native of Annapolis, Maryland, Tameika now resides in the Washington, DC, suburbs with her two daughters, Chandler and London. She enjoys traveling, laughter-filled family time, and what she lovingly calls "indulgent self-care"—a sacred ritual that energizes her pursuit of purpose, wholeness, and unapologetic joy.

Learn more at CultivateToGreat.com.